Wellness at Work

Protecting and promoting employee health and wellbeing

Lynda A. C. Macdonald

Lynda A. C. Macdonald is a self-employed freelance employment law trainer, advisor and writer. She is a panel member of the Employment Tribunal Service in Aberdeen, where she lives.

The Chartered Institute of Personnel and Development is the leading publisher of books and reports for personnel and training professionals, students, and all those concerned with the effective management and development of people at work. For details of all our titles, please contact the publishing department:

Tel: 020 8612 6200

E-mail: publish@cipd.co.uk

The catalogue of all CIPD titles can be viewed on all the CIPD website:

http://www.cipd.co.uk/bookstore

Wellness at Work

Protecting and promoting employee
health and wellbeing

Lynda A. C. Macdonald

Published by the Chartered Institute of Personnel and Development,
151 The Broadway, London SW19 1JQ

First published 2005

© Chartered Institute of Personnel and Development, 2005

The right of Lynda A. C. Macdonald to be identified as author of this Work
has been asserted by her in accordance with sections 77 and 78 of the
Copyright, Designs and Patents Act 1988

Typeset by Curran Publishing Services Ltd

Printed in Great Britain by Cromwell Press, Trowbridge, Wiltshire

British Library Cataloguing in Publication Data

A catalogue of this manual is available from the British Library

ISBN 1 84398 106 8

The views expressed in this manual are the author's own and may
not necessarily reflect those of the CIPD.

The CIPD has made every effort to trace and acknowledge copyright holders. If any source
has been overlooked, CIPD Enterprises would be pleased to redress this for future editions.

Chartered Institute of Personnel and Development,
151 The Broadway, London SW19 1JQ

Tel: 020 8612 6200

E-mail: cipd@cipd.co.uk   Website: www.cipd.co.uk

Incorporated by Royal Charter.   Registered Charity No. 1079797

CONTENTS

LIST OF ACRONYMS

DDP   dismissal and disciplinary procedure
EAT   employment appeals tribunal
ECJ   European Court of Justice
GP   general practitioner (doctor)
HR   human resources
HSE   Health and Safety Executive
IRLR   Industrial Relations Law Reports
SDA   Sex Discrimination Act 1975
SSP   statutory sick pay
UKHL   United Kingdom House of Lords decisions

INTRODUCTION

It is often said that the greatest asset of any organisation is its people. Although something of a cliché, the slogan is still absolutely true of today's workplaces. Yet many employers do not act as if their people were important to them, and do not take positive steps to care for their health or promote their wellbeing. This failure represents a lost opportunity, as staff who feel fit and healthy will be empowered to produce high-quality work, cope well with pressure, and work in partnership with the organisation to achieve its goals. With the ongoing demographic changes in society, an ageing workforce and widespread skills shortages, capable and fit people are becoming a scarce resource and it follows that maximising all employees' value to the organisation must be a high priority for businesses.

The protection and promotion of employees' health and wellbeing can bring considerable advantages not only to the workers, who will enjoy opportunities to improve their own personal levels of health, fitness and wellbeing, but also to employers, who will benefit from increased energy, motivation and productivity in their workforce. Indeed, promoting employees' health and wellbeing is rapidly becoming the single most powerful way of enhancing performance and productivity in order to gain a competitive edge.

'Health' is defined by the World Health Organisation as 'a state of complete physical, mental and social wellbeing, and not merely the absence of disease or infirmity'. This definition makes it clear that health is much more than just the absence of illness and injury. Employers who view the issue of employee health holistically and take positive steps to promote their staff's health and wellbeing, rather than focusing only on employee ill health and rehabilitation, are likely to reap considerable benefits. This is not to say that managing ill-health absence and promoting rehabilitation are not worthwhile goals, but of course (to quote another cliché) prevention is better than cure.

The health and wellbeing of individuals can be influenced substantially by factors at their workplace, and work can be the source of many health problems. The Health and Safety Commission has disclosed that in a single year an estimated 2.3 million people in Britain suffered from an illness that they believed was caused or made worse by their job (or by a past job).

It follows that employers have a valuable role to play in protecting and promoting employees' health and wellbeing, as well as taking steps to reduce or prevent factors that might cause or contribute to ill health, whether physical or mental. Those employers who wish to be seen as socially responsible will have the added satisfaction of knowing that they are investing in improving the nation's health.

This book aims to assist employers to manage the health and wellbeing of their workers. Chapter 1 provides a general discussion on wellness at work, the importance of protecting and promoting employees' health and wellbeing, and the potential effects of not doing so, and the following chapters discuss specific aspects of employee health. Chapter 2 addresses the ever-important topic of workplace stress, primarily from the perspective of prevention, while Chapter 3 takes this topic into the specific area of managing working time and implementing flexible working practices.

Chapter 4 discusses harassment and bullying, two issues that will inevitably damage health, morale and motivation, as well as leading to potentially expensive legal claims if they are not robustly tackled. Chapter 5 addresses the issue of support and rehabilitation for employees who have problems of alcohol or drugs dependency, together with the legal and practical implications of implementing alcohol/drugs screening programmes. Chapter 6 deals with smoking at work and smoking policies.

Chapter 7 addresses long-term ill-health absence in general, including the topics of disability discrimination, mental illness, AIDS and dismissal for long-term ill health, while Chapter 8 follows up by discussing the provision of medical advice and the maintenance of health records, taking into account the provisions of the Human Rights Act 1998, the Data Protection Act 1998 and the Access to Medical Reports Act 1988.   -

Achieving positive improvements in employee health and wellbeing is not a short-term goal. It is best regarded as a journey towards the long-term objective of creating an organisation in which employees are empowered to perform to the very best of their abilities because they are as healthy as they can be and because they feel valued, and thus motivated. All of these outcomes will be advantageous to the employer who will ultimately reap the benefits of a more efficient and productive workforce, with less time off due to sickness, and a consequent reduction in the direct and indirect costs of such absence.

CHAPTER 1

THE IMPORTANCE OF PROTECTING AND PROMOTING EMPLOYEES' HEALTH AND WELLBEING

Introduction

Sickness absence costs UK employers the sum of £11.6 billion a year. This was the finding of a CBI survey on absence and labour turnover, *Counting the Costs*, published in 2003. A CIPD survey on employee absence in the same year revealed that the average level of sickness absence in the United Kingdom amounted to nine working days per employee. Figures produced by the CBI indicate that the average direct cost of employee absence in the public sector is £637 per employee per year, while the equivalent figure in the private sector is £466. If indirect costs such as paying overtime to colleagues to cover an employee's absence are taken into account, these figures shoot up to well over £1,000 per employee per year.

Furthermore, recent government figures showed that incapacity through mental and emotional causes, due partly to work-related stress, is running at more than 200,000 cases each year, and the Health and Safety Commission estimates that 13.4 million days off work were attributed to stress, anxiety or depression in a single year. The CBI has estimated that a third of all sickness absence is due to mental health issues.

Over and above the costs of paying sick pay, organisations whose employees are absent on sick leave suffer loss of productivity, negative impacts on both team working and customer relations, and general disruption to their business, all of which cost dearly in terms of efficiency, and ultimately, profitability. Short-term absences in particular can cause much inconvenience and disruption.

Absences on account of stress-related conditions are increasing every year, and stress is now thought to be the single most common cause of employee absence from work (outstripping the traditional 'bad back'). However, the management of employees' health and wellbeing goes far beyond the single issue of managing stress, notwithstanding the importance of measures implemented to reduce or prevent it in the workplace.

Employers can, and should, be taking positive steps to manage their employees' absences, but should also be implementing measures to promote their wellness, thus minimising the likelihood of absences occurring in the first place.

What is wellness management?

Adopting a policy of wellness management means taking a holistic approach towards the promotion of employees' health and wellbeing in order to create enhanced business performance. Wellness management is about the prevention of sickness and absence, rather than rehabilitation. It is about positively managing the healthy so that they are less likely to fall sick, rather than just managing the sick. Clearly no employer can prevent all employee illnesses or absences, but proactive management and health initiatives in the workplace can do much to reduce their number and frequency, especially casual absences of one or two days.

One of the biggest problems for employers is the gnawing impact (and potentially high costs) of low-level, chronic conditions such as back pain, which may cause frequent absenteeism and thus erode the organisation's efficiency and productivity. Such problems cannot be effectively addressed by the provision of sick pay or medical insurance alone, but may be alleviated considerably by active wellness management.

Managing employees' health and wellbeing is thus about positively promoting the health and wellbeing of all employees, encouraging and helping them to feel fitter and look better. The health of the workforce – both physical and psychological – will be a major contributor to the success (or otherwise) of the business, and is largely untapped as a means of enhancing organisational performance and gaining competitive advantage.

Management responsibilities

Clearly, any initiative to manage and promote employees' health and wellbeing must have full management support and commitment. This will, of course, include adhering to both the spirit and the letter of the law, including both statutory legislation and common law, including the common law duty of care.

The common law duty of care

Every employee's contract of employment includes a range of implied terms: duties that are incorporated into the contract as a result of common law principles (that is, decisions of courts and appeal tribunals).

One of the main implied duties that place obligations on employers is the duty to take reasonable care of employees' health and safety, with the term 'health' incorporating mental health. This common law duty means that employers owe their employees a duty in common law not to cause them foreseeable harm by acting negligently or omitting to act to protect them from foreseeable harm.

The common law duty of care dates back to 1932 when the famous case of *Donoghue v Stevenson [1932] AC 532, [1932] All ER Rep 1*, was determined. This case involved an individual who discovered a snail in a glass of ginger beer, causing her to suffer considerable psychological trauma. The case established the principle that everyone has a general duty of care not to injure, by act or omission, any other person who might reasonably foreseeably suffer an injury as a result of their act or omission. The common law duty of care has come to be implied (i.e. automatically incorporated) in every employment contract regardless of what, if any, written documentation (for example policy statements) dealing with health and safety exists within the organisation.

The existence of the duty of care means that, if employees suffer any injury (whether physical or psychological) to their health at work as a result of a breach of the implied duty, they can either sue their employer for damages for personal injury, or resign and claim constructive dismissal on the basis that their employer has acted in fundamental breach of their contract of employment (see Chapter 2 under 'The potential consequences for the employer of workplace stress').

Common causes of employee absences

There are many causes of employee absence, which will fall broadly under three headings:

- personal characteristics and attitudes

- factors in the workplace

- external factors.

Personal characteristics and attitudes

Every manager understands that individual employees vary in their attitudes to their work and to the organisation. Individual attitudes can be an important factor affecting employee attendance, as there will be a greater tendency to take a day off on account of a minor problem where an employee's general attitude to his or her employment is negative.

Many other personal characteristics, such as age, gender, job role and length of service will affect attendance in general. Past behaviour in relation to attendance will usually be a sound predictor of future reliability.

Factors in the workplace

Issues that will affect employee attendance and absence include the way work is organised and carried out, physical working conditions, the employer's policies, procedures and rules (and the degree of flexibility in these), the degree of stress inherent in the employee's job, the existence of any unresolved conflict and above all management attitude and approach towards staff, especially that of the employee's immediate line manager or supervisor.

External factors

A range of external factors, beyond both the employer's and the employees' control, will inevitably affect employees' attendance at work. These include economic and market conditions: evidence demonstrates that rates of absenteeism decline markedly when 'times are tight'. Other factors affecting attendance may include family circumstances and the degree to which an individual has caring responsibilities for children or elderly relatives. The impact of these on absence levels can be reduced substantially if the employer operates flexible working practices and discourages a long-hours culture (see Chapter 3).

A CIPD survey conducted in 2001 (*Employee Absence: A Survey of Management Policy and Practice*) showed that between a third and a half of all short-term absences relate to genuine illness or accident. This suggests, conversely, that more than half of short-term absences are not due to genuine sickness. Other reasons for absence may of course be genuine, for example if an employee's child suddenly falls ill, but nevertheless there would appear to be considerable scope for employers to seek improvements.

In general, a high proportion of an organisation's overall absences will be attributable to a small percentage of the workforce. By applying sound proactive techniques to promote employees' health and wellbeing, that small percentage of people is likely to become smaller in the course of time.

Health initiatives

In the census of 2001, almost 10 per cent of the population of England and Wales stated that their health was 'not good'. With an ageing population and the advent of age discrimination legislation in 2006, employers will need to learn to manage the health and wellbeing of older workers who, statistically, are less likely than their younger counterparts to be in their physical and mental prime.

Employers may wish to consider a range of health initiatives to promote the health and wellbeing of their workers, including older ones. The following list is not intended to be prescriptive, but rather to offer some suggestions as to how enlightened employers might protect and promote their employees' health and wellbeing. The list is not in any particular order.

- Encourage employees who smoke to give up the habit, perhaps by offering an incentive to anyone who succeeds in giving up and remaining free from cigarettes for a defined minimum period (for example six months).

- Offer the opportunity for employees who declare a wish to give up smoking to obtain support and counselling (preferably during working hours).

- Ensure than any in-house restaurant or canteen facility offers only good-quality, healthy food and minimises the availability of high-fat and 'junk' foods.

- Ensure that any in-house restaurant or canteen facility offers at least one attractively presented low-calorie meal each day.

- Encourage the providers of on-site food to publicise the calorie and fat content of each meal/snack on offer.

- Consider offering free fruit to all staff two or three times a week.

- Introduce 'theme days', for example a healthy heart day.

- Provide interesting and challenging information about relevant health issues such as healthy eating, dieting and exercise, for example on noticeboards or on a company intranet.

- As with employees who succeed in giving up smoking, offer an incentive to any employee who succeeds in losing an agreed amount of weight, subject to the proviso that the agreed weight loss is maintained for a minimum period.

- Employ a wellness coach to offer confidential practical help and advice to individual employees during working hours.

- Bring in a qualified instructor to run short fitness and exercise sessions, either at lunchtimes or at the end of the official working day (or both).

- Arrange lunch-time walks.

- Offer occasional free in-house seminars on health and wellness.

- Offer staff the opportunity to have a yearly personalised, private assessment of their health and lifestyle, together with advice on nutrition, exercise, stress, blood pressure, cholesterol and the like.

- Offer employees the opportunity for a free, annual, full medical check with an occupational doctor or nurse, the results of which are to be regarded as confidential. This should also include an opportunity for employees to ask questions about specific health issues or raise any concerns they may have.

- Offer employees discounted membership at a local gym or health and fitness centre of their choice.

- Introduce (in conjunction with an occupational health professional) a rehabilitation programme for staff with health problems such as mental illness or dependence on alcohol/drugs.

- Provide a free and confidential telephone help-line that staff can access at any time to obtain counselling in relation to both work-related and personal problems.

- Conduct risk assessments and occasional attitude surveys in relation to workplace stress and its causes (see Chapter 2).

- Offer flexible working whenever possible to any member of staff who wants it (see Chapter 3).

- Introduce and operate an anti-harassment/bullying policy and an accompanying complaints procedure (see Chapter 4).

- Offer support, appropriate medical treatment and counselling to any employees who acknowledge that they have a problem with dependence on alcohol or drugs, in order to help them rehabilitate (see Chapter 5).

- Offer support and counselling for any employee who is known to be HIV positive or have AIDS (see Chapter 7).

Consulting staff

Rather than implementing initiatives unilaterally, an employer would do well to consult staff about what health and wellness measures they would personally value. Different individuals will need and want different things at different stages of their lives. A flexible programme, where each employee can opt for one or more benefits, is likely to work best. Essentially, the employer should ensure that all workplace health and wellbeing initiatives are based on information and feedback received from employees.

Motivation and morale and their potential impact on the business

High levels of absenteeism can have a substantial negative impact on employee motivation and morale. Equally, research indicates that in organisations where morale is already low, people are more likely to take occasional days off work as a form of avoidance behaviour. The issues of low morale and high absenteeism can thus evolve into a vicious circle with the one aggravating the other. Similarly an employee with a relatively minor ailment that does not strictly justify time off work may actively choose to stay away (if factors at work in general are demotivating), while an employee who is generally happy at work may, in similar circumstances, elect to attend. In other words, unhappy employees are much more likely to be absent from work for short periods.

It is therefore advisable, as part of a holistic approach towards health and wellbeing at work, for employers to pay attention to the wide range of factors that can motivate or demotivate employees and affect levels of job satisfaction. A discussion of such factors is outside the scope of this book, but there are many excellent publications that address the subject.

In February 2003, the CIPD produced an action plan for employers working towards occupational health and organisational effectiveness. They recommended that such an action plan should include:

- strong leadership

- employee involvement

- a clear mission statement

- a health and safety policy addressing prevention, wellness and partnership

- a clear picture of how resources are determined and responsibilities are assigned

- auditing

- benchmarking

- planning for improvements

- goals and targets

- a strategy review and monitoring process with associated time-scales.

In-house occupational health

Larger organisations may wish to consider introducing an in-house health and medical facility for employees. Such provision can be as simple or sophisticated as the employer sees fit, and can be particularly effective if a large number of employees are working on a single site. In some parts of Britain, access to a GP has become difficult, with people often having to wait days or even weeks for an appointment. The availability of an occupational doctor at the workplace, so that employees can make appointments and be seen promptly, is likely to reduce the need for absenteeism.

The main role of occupational health should, however, be to prevent illness and injury and to promote good health among the workforce. An occupational doctor can work with the employer to anticipate the likely risks to health at the workplace and put measures in place to prevent or at least reduce the likelihood of ill health.

For smaller organisations, the alternative may be an online or telephone provision. Clearly this is not as beneficial as the opportunity to consult a doctor face to face, but is nevertheless a benefit for employees and a feature that might help to promote health awareness and reduce absenteeism.

Benefits for employees

An in-house medical facility could provide some or all of the following benefits for employees:

- access to an occupational doctor for full health assessment and medical examinations, and/or to an occupational nurse for routine advice and health monitoring

- advice for employees who travel overseas on the health issues that might affect them at their destination, together with the provision of vaccinations and immunisations

- provision of dental care

- routine eye examinations

- physiotherapy, chiropractic and osteopathy to treat musculoskeletal disorders

- provision of advice on ergonomics for individuals at work, for example advice on posture and workstation design

- provision of stress counselling.

Whatever facilities are offered, the employer should take steps to market them effectively to employees, otherwise they may be underused.

Benefits for employers

Over and above the obvious benefits to staff, employers are likely to gain from lower levels of sickness absence. They will also benefit from having direct access to advice about individual employees' fitness (or otherwise) to perform their jobs, and about any work adjustments that might be appropriate for an employee with a particular medical condition or disability. Furthermore an occupational doctor would be able to play a key role in conducting risk assessments, by ensuring that the assessments take full account of any health hazards at the workplace, helping to devise and implement controls to minimise such risks and providing important advice on any pre-existing condition an employee may have that makes him or her more vulnerable than usual to harm arising from conditions in the workplace.

An occupational doctor can also provide pre-employment screening to ensure prospective job applicants are sufficiently fit to perform the jobs for which they are being considered.

The availability of in-house occupational health scheme will reduce the amount of time off that staff would otherwise need to attend external appointments. For example, if an employee with back pain can obtain physiotherapy on site, this might mean a half hour off work rather than the half day or so that could be needed to attend an external appointment.

Healthcare insurance

Healthcare cover of various types has always been one of the most highly valued employment benefits. Various type of benefit can be offered, the main ones being:

- Payment of sick pay: the employer continues to pay the employee's wage/salary for a defined period of time.

- Permanent health insurance: a contract with an outside provider under which, if employees are incapable of performing their work due to illness or injury, the provider pays a defined percentage of their wage or salary once absence has exceeded an agreed number of months.

- Private medical insurance: the employer provides employees (and possibly their partners/children as well) cover under a group scheme so that they may obtain private health care in defined circumstances up to a defined limit.

Provision of one or more of these benefits has one key advantage: it will make employees feel more secure and confident, removing any worry about money difficulties in the event of illness or injury. Additionally, because NHS treatment may often involve long waiting lists, the provision of private medical insurance will give employees the comfort of knowing that, if they develop a non life-threatening condition that may nevertheless cause them considerable pain and discomfort, they can obtain treatment for that condition simply, quickly and without cost to themselves.

These benefits, although to be recommended, do not address the underlying causes of employee sickness and absence. Furthermore, the second and third – permanent health insurance and private medical insurance – will not help the employer manage or reduce routine, short-term ailments and casual absenteeism. Positive measures to promote employee health and wellbeing are required to achieve that goal (see 'Health initiatives' above).

The benefits of initiatives to promote employees' health and wellbeing

The benefits of taking steps to promote employees' health and wellbeing can be summed up in one very simple sentence. Healthy employees will be fit to build a healthy organisation. The opposite is also true of course: if employees are sick, lethargic or generally unhealthy, they will not be able to work to the full extent of their capabilities, thus preventing the organisation from reaching its full potential.

Implementing positive health and wellbeing initiatives is thus a sound business investment, although the results can be hard to measure and will often be long term rather than immediate. Thus, it is probably not realistic to expect to obtain an exact measurement of, for example, how many instances of absenteeism could have been prevented in the past year if the employer had introduced measures to promote employees' health and wellbeing. The matter is largely one of common sense and may have to be taken on trust.

One immediate benefit for employers, however, will arise from the fact that employees who are offered a programme of health promotion at work are likely to feel that they are important to the company. Making employees feeling that they are genuinely valued as individuals is the key to positive motivation, which in turn is the vital ingredient necessary if the organisation seeks high-level performance and productivity from its staff.

Some of the other benefits of implementing policies and incentives to protect and promote employees' health and wellbeing could be:

- a tool to aid recruitment, especially in today's competitive markets, since an organisation that provides health benefits and incentives will become an employer of choice

- an aid to retention because employees will value and respect the fact that their employer cares about their wellbeing, and will thus be less likely to seek alternative employment

- a reduction in employee stress and all its associated problems

- a positive way of ensuring that the organisation fully meets its duty of care

- a reduction in direct and indirect costs, such as overtime payments for staff to cover for a colleague's sickness absence, or training for a replacement employee

- as stated above, people are likely to be happier at work, which in turn leads to better performance and greater productivity.

Costs versus benefits to the business

Obviously there is a cost element involved in implementing any type of health promotion programme or health/wellness initiative, but it can be argued that the cost will be a secure investment that will provide a payback considerably greater than the amount of money spent. This is because the positive promotion of employees' health through the types of incentive detailed above (under 'Health initiatives') will help to prevent sickness and absence. Sickness absence is a major cost to employers in Britain – £11.6 billion a year according to the CBI absence and labour turnover survey, *Counting the Costs*.

Furthermore, it is strongly arguable that health and wellbeing programmes are about empowering individuals to work to the best of their abilities, thus increasing the organisation's productivity and hence profitability.

In any event, employers may wish to consider both the direct and indirect costs of not implementing initiatives to protect and promote health and wellbeing in the workplace. While the direct costs of sick pay can and should be measured and monitored, indirect costs are harder to quantify. They can include:

- negative impacts on work efficiency

- general disruption to work processes

- loss of productivity

- lower staff morale when the colleagues of an absent employee are expected to take on extra work

- overtime payments to cover the work of an absent employee

- the time and cost of procuring a temporary replacement for someone who is off work

- the time and cost of training that replacement

- the potential need for additional supervision of a replacement employee

- difficulties in maintaining effective customer relationships and consequent loss of goodwill

- the increased possibility of mistakes or inconsistency in advice to customers

- increased insurance premiums.

Matters can be summed up succinctly in the Health and Safety Executive's slogan, 'Good Health is Good Business'.

POINTS TO NOTE

- Employers whose staff are often absent on sick leave suffer loss of productivity, negative impacts on both team working and customer relations and general disruption to their business.

- Wellness management is about the prevention of sickness and absence, rather than rehabilitation; put another way, it is about positively managing the healthy so that they are less likely to fall sick, rather than just managing the sick.

- High levels of absenteeism can have a substantial negative impact on motivation and morale and, equally, the existence of low morale can increase the incidence of employee absence.

- The main role of occupational health should be to prevent illness and injury and to promote good health among the workforce.

- An in-house medical facility has many benefits for employees, including the provision of access to an occupational doctor for health checks and routine advice, as well as the possibility of specialist areas of care such as dentistry, physiotherapy and stress counselling.

- The availability of in-house occupational health schemes will reduce the amount of time off work that employees would otherwise need to attend external appointments.

- Although healthcare insurance has always been one of the most valued of employment benefits, it does not address the underlying causes of employee sickness and absence.

- Implementing positive health and wellbeing initiatives is a sound business investment, although the results can be hard to measure and will often be long term rather than immediate.

- Policies and incentives to protect and promote employees' health and wellbeing confer many benefits, for example by aiding recruitment and retention, reducing employee stress and cutting the direct and indirect costs associated with absences.

ACTION POINTS

- Recognise that many factors in the workplace will affect employee attendance and absence, including physical working conditions, the employer's policies and procedures (and the degree of flexibility in these), the degree of stress inherent in the employee's job, and above all management attitude and approach towards staff.

- Give consideration to a range of possible health initiatives.

- Introduce measures to assist staff who wish to give up smoking.

- Take steps to encourage employees to improve their diet.

- Employ a wellness coach to offer confidential practical help and advice to individual employees, and a qualified fitness instructor to run short fitness and exercise sessions at the workplace.

- Offer staff the opportunity to have a yearly health assessment and general health/fitness advice with an occupational health doctor or nurse.

- Provide a free and confidential telephone help-line that staff can access at any time to obtain counselling in relation to both work-related and personal problems.

- Consult staff about what health and wellness measures they would personally value.

- Introduce an in-house health and medical facility for employees if possible, or alternatively (for smaller employers) provide an online or telephone facility.

- Recognise that employees who are offered a programme of health promotion at work are likely to feel valued and that this in turn is the key to positive motivation, which is the vital ingredient necessary if the organisation seeks high-level performance and productivity from its staff.

- Consider both the direct and indirect costs of not implementing initiatives to protect and promote employees' health and wellbeing, which may include negative impacts on work efficiency, general disruption to work processes, lower staff morale, difficulties in maintaining effective customer relationships and extra costs.

CHAPTER 2

PREVENTING AND MANAGING WORKPLACE STRESS

Introduction

Workplace stress is an issue that competent employers cannot afford to ignore. It was reported in *People Management* in March 2003 that in the year 2001–2, workers took a total of 13 million days off work as a direct result of work-related stress, anxiety or depression, which represented almost a third of all working days' sick leave over the same period. As we noted in Chapter 1, the Health and Safety Commission estimated the figure at 13.4 million days per year, and the CBI agreed with *People Management*'s assessment that a third of all sickness absences were due to these causes. If employers wish to take the subject of employees' health and wellbeing seriously, it will be important for them to take positive measures to tackle workplace stress.

Stress prevention and control is an essential part of the effective management of people at work. Denying that workplace stress exists, or adopting an unsympathetic or macho response to it, will be unhelpful to say the least, and may lead to the exacerbation of any existing workplace problems. For example, if management assume that workplace stress is not an issue for their organisation, or that employees who appear unable to cope with the pressures of working life are 'wimps' or 'not good enough', then the likely consequences for the business could be:

- poor job performance and consequent loss of productivity, leading to delays to schedules because of frequent and persistent absences from work

- high costs in the form of statutory and contractual sick pay

- negative impacts on customer relationships

- low morale and motivation generally, especially if increasing pressure is piled onto other employees who have to cope with an absent colleague's workload on top of their own

- high levels of complaints and grievances, which in turn will drain management time and resources

- increased rate of accidents or near-miss incidents, since an employee who is suffering from stress may be more liable to cause, or be involved in, accidents

- the risk of legal claims against the organisation.

Many organisations have, over the years, cut their staff numbers to minimum levels. One result is that many employees have much higher workloads than in the past. At the same time, employers demand higher levels of performance and commitment from their employees at all levels of the organisation. A combination of long working hours, tight deadlines and intense work demands often combine to produce high levels of pressure on staff, which in turn can intensify workplace stress.

Stress, therefore, needs to be recognised as an important management issue, and addressed in a positive and constructive manner with a view to prevention or reduction whenever possible. Furthermore, managers need to be constantly alert to the possibility of harmful levels of stress among their employees, and ready to take appropriate remedial action as soon as a potential problem is identified. A sympathetic and supportive approach is paramount if the organisation is to avoid the negative consequences identified above.

The effective management of stress will pay dividends for the organisation because such management will increase employee motivation and productivity, reduce absenteeism and promote safety. It will therefore inevitably enhance the company's profitability. The commitment to positive stress management must, of course, exist at the top level of management, and this commitment should be cascaded down throughout the organisation.

What is stress?

Stress on its own is not recognised as a medical condition, nor will an employee have grounds for any type of legal claim against an employer on account of being placed under a moderate degree of pressure at work, even if that pressure causes some stress. Most jobs create some stress for the people doing them, and it is generally accepted that a moderate level of stress is beneficial as a healthy stimulant to help people deal with challenging situations at work. Where, however, pressures of work become excessive in relation to the individual's ability to cope, the result may be a level of stress that is likely to cause the employee harm. In particular, if stress is intense, constant, and/or endured over a lengthy period of time, it may lead to physical or mental illness. Where this happens, the employer may be held liable (see below under 'Legal consequences').

Just as stress is not a medically recognised condition, it has no legal definition either. However, the Health and Safety Executive has provided a helpful definition, which is: 'the reaction people have to excessive pressures or other types of demand placed on them'. Stress is therefore the body's reaction (whether mental or physical) to an actual or perceived imbalance between the demands being placed on the person, and that person's individual coping resources.

An important point to bear in mind is that, when it comes to coping with stress, people differ widely. One person may cope admirably with heavy workloads, long hours and intense pressure while another, performing similar work under similar conditions, may crack under the strain. Such a situation does not mean that the second individual is weak or incapable but merely that he or she is different from the first. It is distinctly unhelpful for any manager to say: 'What's the matter with you? Everyone else copes with the pressures of the job.' It should never be assumed that just because one employee copes competently with a particular workload, another employee should automatically be capable of doing the same.

Instead, it is important to recognise that stress is not dependent only on the amount of workplace pressure, but will result from an imbalance between the amount of pressure placed on an individual employee and that employee's personal ability to cope with it. Furthermore, someone might be able to cope adequately with a relatively high level of workplace pressure at a particular time, but at a different time in his or her life might crumble under the same amount of pressure. This may be due to factors present in the individual's personal life at different times.

Common causes of workplace stress

There are many potential causes of workplace stress. The most common are:

- Heavy workloads, especially when accompanied by unrealistic targets and/or tight deadlines, sometimes imposed as a result of customer demands that are perceived as unreasonable or unachievable.

- The nature of the job or type of work. Specific problems could include poor task design, repetitive and/or boring work, lack of clarity in relation to goals, priorities and duties, a perception that the work is meaningless or unimportant, lack of control over the work and the way it is done, and lack of opportunity for the employee to use his or her skills.

- Long or unsocial working hours (see Chapter 3).

- Lack of appropriate training, particularly when an employee is transferred or promoted into a job with different responsibilities and duties.

- Lack of management support, for example when someone is required to take on responsibility without being given the necessary authority or control.

- Job insecurity. Takeovers, mergers and business reorganisations lead frequently to restructuring, redundancies and flatter management hierarchies. Few jobs are secure in the world of business today and the notion of a 'job for life' is long gone.

- Change very often makes people feel uncomfortable and anxious at the very least, and seriously stressed to the point of illness at worst.

- Lack of communication. The uncertainty, fear and sense of isolation caused by lack of information should never be underestimated as potential sources of stress at work.

- Too much communication. For example, there may be huge volumes of irrelevant e-mails as a result of the employer having no policy or guidelines on use of e-mail and the Internet.

- Management style. A persistent authoritarian management style, for example, can stifle initiative, cause resentment and create stress in those who are its victims, while a more open, communicative and consultative style is more likely to prevent and/or reduce stress levels within the team.

- Poor or difficult relationships with colleagues or customers, whether on a professional or personal level.

- Harassment or bullying (see Chapter 4).

- Environmental factors, such as noise, poor ventilation, unsatisfactory temperature control or cramped conditions.

Signs and symptoms that an employee may be suffering from stress

Although managers and supervisors cannot be expected to be experts on the subject of workplace stress, they should be alert to the possibility of their staff developing stress-related symptoms, which may be caused by factors at work. Some such symptoms are:

- a gradual deterioration in job performance, conduct or even attitude to work for no apparent reason

- uncharacteristic or irrational behaviour, such as unexplained moodiness in someone who is normally easy-going, lack of patience in someone who is normally patient or uncharacteristic outbreaks of anger

- increased absenteeism or lateness

- increased use of cigarettes, coffee or alcohol

- excessive hours spent at work, coupled with an apparent unwillingness to take time off

- difficulty in concentrating or remembering

- indecision or difficulty in making decisions

- over-reaction to trivial matters

- lack of attention to detail, leading to an increase in mistakes

- constant fatigue, frequent headaches or other unexplained physical aches and pains

- lack of attention to personal appearance or personal hygiene.

The main indicator will usually be an unexplained change in someone's behaviour or work performance, for example where a usually reliable employee starts to make lots of mistakes without any obvious explanation for the change.

Whatever it is that is causing such symptoms will be a problem not only for the employee but also for management, in that the employee's performance or conduct at work will invariably be adversely affected. Clearly though, the symptoms listed above may be due to factors other than stress, and the manager should not imagine that he or she can automatically diagnose the employee's apparent ailment effectively. Instead one should consider the context and overall environment in which the symptoms appear.

Since workplace stress is a management responsibility, the onus will be on the manager of anyone who shows signs of possible stress to initiate action to discuss the symptoms, with a view to offering support where possible. If nothing is done, the problem may persist and the employee's general health may deteriorate.

Why an employee may be reluctant to admit to stress

It does not take much intelligence to realise that an employee who is suffering from stress at work may be reluctant to come forward and admit that he or she is not coping with the demands of the job. Such employees may:

- fear that they will be perceived as incompetent or inadequate if they admit to an inability to cope with workplace pressures

- be embarrassed about admitting that they feel stressed out

- feel that to burden their manager with their problems would be inappropriate

- feel guilty about the notion of being unable to cope, or worried that they may be letting their manager down

- worry that they may lose out on promotion opportunities, or even be dismissed, if they admit they are not coping.

It may even be that some employees are unwilling or unable to recognise that they are suffering from stress or that the level of stress they are experiencing is in danger of damaging their health.

It is the responsibility of every manager who observes symptoms such as those listed above (see 'Signs and symptoms that an employee may be suffering from stress') to encourage employees to speak openly about how they feel and about the causes of their stress, and to seek solutions to combat the problem. It would be naïve and foolish for any manager to imagine, just because no one has come forward to complain, that the problem of workplace stress does not exist.

The potential consequences for the employer of workplace stress

Employers who do not bother to take steps to prevent and manage workplace stress are likely to face a number of negative consequences, both practical and legal.

Practical consequences

Even if an employee's levels of stress do not appear to be having a serious effect on that person's productivity, the stress may still result in minor ailments such as poor sleep patterns leading to fatigue, difficulty in concentrating and a state of general anxiety or worry. This is bound to have a detrimental effect on the employee's ability to perform effectively at work in the longer term. Such ailments may also lead to frequent short-term absences from work, which are in the interests of neither employer nor employee. Furthermore, continuation of the stress over a longer period may lead on to more serious problems, such as longer-term illness.

Legal consequences

There are a number of possible legal consequences for employers who do not effectively manage workplace stress. These can be summarised as follows:

- claims for damages for personal injury (see below under 'When an employee may seek damages for personal injury')

- claims for constructive dismissal from workers who resign as a direct result of a breach of the employer's duty of care, or a breach of the implied duty of trust and confidence (see below under 'The possibility of a constructive dismissal claim')

- liability under discrimination legislation for claims of disability discrimination if work-related stress leads to a long-term mental illness that can be classed as a disability under the Disability Discrimination Act 1995

- criminal liability under the Health and Safety at Work Act 1974.

When an employee may seek damages for personal injury

Most people understand the logic behind the principle that an employee who is physically injured at work or develops an industrial illness as a result of negligence on the part of an employer can bring a claim to court for damages for personal injury. This same principle applies to claims for psychiatric injury, although a claim of this type is undoubtedly harder to prove. This is because the 'injury' may not be visible or easily definable in medical terms, and it may not be easy to establish that it was caused by factors in the workplace as opposed to aspects of the employee's personal life.

It is important to bear in mind that where anyone is injured at work as a result of an employee's negligence, the employer will be vicariously liable for the negligent act of the person who caused the injury, provided the action that caused the injury was perpetrated in the course of employment. It follows that an employee who suffers a psychiatric injury as a consequence of negligence will tend to sue the employer for damages, rather than the individual who caused the stress that led to the injury. Nevertheless a claim may also be brought against an employee who acted negligently, for example the manager of the person who suffered the injury.

The key issues involved in a claim for psychiatric injury are:

- whether the employer negligently breached the implied duty of care

- whether the employee has suffered an injury (that is, a recognised psychiatric illness)

- whether the employee's injury was caused by the employer's negligence (as opposed to factors in the employee's personal life)

- whether the injury to the employee's mental health was reasonably foreseeable.

Whether the employer negligently breached the implied duty of care

In order to have a chance of succeeding in a claim for damages for personal injury, the employee would have to show that the employer had acted negligently and breached the common law duty of care. A key point to note is that negligence in this context is not about everyday carelessness, but rather about whether the employer failed to take reasonable steps to prevent reasonably foreseeable harm to the employee's health. The duty of care is discussed further in Chapter 1.

Whether the employee has suffered an injury

Employers may take heart in the fact that stress on its own will not constitute an 'injury' for the purposes of a personal injury claim by an employee. For example, in the case of *Fraser v State Hospitals Board for Scotland [2000] IRLR 672*, the Scottish Court of Session held that the duty of care owed by an employer does not involve a duty to protect employees from 'unpleasant emotions' such as grief, anger and resentment, or 'normal human conditions' such as anxiety or stress where these do not involve any form of psychiatric injury. In contrast, however, if the employee's stress has caused a recognised mental illness to develop, then it will be possible for a claim to be made out. Detailed medical evidence would be required to satisfy the court that the employee had developed such an illness.

Causation

The 'test of causation' can be a difficult hurdle for an employee to overcome in court, as stress leading to an injury to heath is often the result of an accumulation of different pressures. It does not, however, have to be proved 'beyond reasonable doubt' that the illness was caused by factors in the workplace, which would most likely be impossible in most cases. Instead, the outcome of the case will be based on the 'balance of probabilities test': whether it is more likely than not (in the opinion of the court) that factors in the workplace caused the employee to become ill, or materially increased the risk of injury to health.

Foreseeability

The employee must also convince a court that the injury to health was something the employer could have, or should reasonably have, foreseen. If harm is reasonably foreseeable and employers do nothing to prevent it, they will be guilty of negligence and liable for damages.

In the light of increasing media exposure being given to stress at work, and to increasing medical knowledge about the link between stress and illness, it is likely to become correspondingly more difficult for employers to argue that they could not have reasonably foreseen that an employee might become ill as a result of stress caused by severe workplace pressures.

Case law

The first case in which an employee sought damages for injury to mental health was the highly-publicised case of *Walker v Northumberland County Council [1995] IRLR 35* (see 'Key case 1' in the box below).

Since the *Walker* case, there have been a number of further legal developments.

In four cases dealt with together by the Court of Appeal in 2002 [*Sutherland (Chairman of the Governors of St Thomas Becket RC High School) v Hatton, Barber v Somerset County Council, Sandwell Metropolitan Borough Council v Jones* and *Baker Refractories Ltd v Melvyn Edward Bishop [2002] IRLR 263*], the court provided some useful guidance on the factors that are relevant when considering whether or not an employer should be held liable for an employee's psychiatric injury. The general principles are that:

- Unless the risk of harm to the particular employee from occupational stress is reasonably foreseeable, the employer will not be liable.

- Foreseeability depends on what the employer knows, or ought reasonably to know, about the individual employee.

Key case 1

Walker v Northumberland County Council [1995] IRLR 35

Mr Walker was a social worker whose job involved dealing with cases of child abuse. His workload had been steadily increasing over a number of years, and eventually he suffered a nervous breakdown. When, the following year, he had recovered sufficiently to return to work, he was promised additional resources and support, but in practice these did not materialise. Instead his workload and responsibility increased further and he suffered a second nervous breakdown six months later. Mr Walker subsequently sued the Council for damages for personal injury, arguing that the Council was in breach of its duty of care to provide a safe working environment.

The court found that the Council could not be held liable for Mr Walker's first breakdown as, in their view, they could not have reasonably foreseen that he was exposed to a significant risk of harm to health as a result of his workload. However, in relation to the second breakdown, the court held that, in light of the fact that Mr Walker had already had one breakdown, the Council could have reasonably foreseen that he would suffer another, given that the size of workload and types of pressures that had led to the first breakdown had continued. The Council was thus in breach of its duty of care by failing to provide effective support to alleviate Mr Walker's workload and the stress it was causing him.

Mr Walker was eventually awarded an out-of-court settlement of £175,000, although there was no admission of liability and so the case did not create a binding legal precedent.

- Whether or not an injury is reasonably foreseeable will depend on the relationship between the demands of the particular job and the particular characteristics of the employee.

- Relevant factors include:
  - the nature and extent of the work (for example whether the workload is much greater than normal, or is particularly demanding intellectually or emotionally)
  - whether the demands on the employee are unreasonable when compared to others
  - whether there are signs that other employees doing the same work are suffering harmful levels of stress
  - whether there is an abnormal level of sickness or absenteeism
  - whether there are signs from a particular employee of impending harm to health (such as past illness attributable to stress, frequent or prolonged stress-related absences, or complaints or warnings from the employee or from others about stress).

- Employers are entitled to assume that an individual employee can withstand the normal pressures of the job, unless they know, or ought to know, of some particular problem or vulnerability.

- A particular vulnerability could be assumed if, for example, the employee has had frequent or prolonged absences from work attributable to stress, or has complained to management about the harmful effects of workplace stress.

- There is no obligation on the employer to make intrusive enquiries, and an employer is generally entitled to take what an employee says at face value.

The court's key conclusion was that the duty to take steps to prevent harm arises only when signs that a particular employee might suffer psychiatric illness as a result of workplace stress are so plain that any reasonable employer would realise that something should be done about it. If at that point reasonable steps to prevent harm are not taken, the employer will be liable.

The court also stated, interestingly, that an employer who offers a confidential advice service to its employees, with referral to appropriate counselling or treatment, is unlikely to be found to be in breach of the duty to take care.

Following on from the Court of Appeal decisions above, one of the claimants appealed his case to the House of Lords. The appealed case, *Barber v Somerset County Council [2004] UKHL 13*, was determined in 2004 (see 'Key case 2' in the box below).

This House of Lords ruling in effect puts the onus on the employer to investigate at the point at which the employee notifies them that there is a problem. 'Notification' in this

Key case 2

Barber v Somerset County Council [2004] UKHL 13

The facts of the case were that Mr Barber was Head of Maths at a secondary school, and was regularly working between 61 and 70 hours a week. He began to suffer from stress, and was signed off sick for three weeks. He filled in a sickness form stating that his problem was 'over-stressed-depression' and the form was counter-signed by one of the deputy head teachers. He also complained to the school management, but was told that all the staff were under stress, and nothing was done to help him. In November of the same year, he had a breakdown. Later he retired on medical advice, having suffered a series of depressive illnesses.

The case turned on whether the Council had breached their duty of care towards Mr Barber. The House of Lords found that the case was a borderline one, but upheld it. They judged that once the certificate indicating stress had come to the school's attention, senior management should 'at the very least, have taken the initiative in making sympathetic enquires about Mr Barber when he returned to work, and made some reduction in his workload to ease his return.... Even a small reduction in his duties, coupled with the feeling that the senior management team was on his side, might be itself have made a real difference. ... Mr Barber's condition should have been monitored, and if it did not improve, some drastic action would have had to be taken.'

Mr Barber was awarded £72,547 damages for personal injury.

context could be held to have occurred as a result of the provision of a sick note specifying 'stress', 'anxiety' or 'depression', or could of course take place through the employee raising the matter with a manager. Following an investigation, the employer should, if it is established that the employee is vulnerable to stress-related illness, be prepared to take appropriate measures to reduce his or her stress levels, for example by adjusting the workload. To say that 'everyone is under pressure' will not be a satisfactory response.

An employer cannot defend a claim for stress-related personal injury by arguing that the employee was unusually susceptible or vulnerable to stress or illness, or that the employer was unaware of any such special vulnerability. It is a fact of life that some people are more susceptible to stress than others and different people have different coping resources.

Damages for injury to health as part of a claim for unlawful discrimination

In determining claims for discrimination (including claims for harassment) on grounds of sex, race, religion or belief, sexual orientation or disability, employment tribunals have the authority to award damages for personal injury caused by the discrimination. This principle, confirmed initially in the case of *Sherrif v Klyne Tugs (Lowestoft) Ltd [1999] IRLR 481*, means that if an employee has become ill as a direct result of harassment (or any other form of discrimination) that occurred in the course of employment, that person can claim additional compensation over and above that for financial loss and injury to feelings. The tribunal will address whether, on the basis of medical evidence, the employee's condition amounts to a psychiatric injury, and if so whether the injury was directly attributable to the discrimination. If, following that assessment, the tribunal considers it just and equitable to do so, they may, at their discretion award damages to the employee.

In *Essa v Laing Ltd [2004] IRLR 313*, the Court of Appeal ruled that in such a case, the employee who has suffered the psychiatric injury does not have to show that it was reasonably foreseeable that he or she would become ill (instead it is accepted that discriminatory treatment, and especially harassment at work, should automatically be viewed as likely to cause stress-related illness). The employee has to show only that the injury was caused by the harassment or other discriminatory treatment.

In contrast, damages for injury to health on account of an employee's dismissal, or the manner of the dismissal, are not recoverable in law.

The possibility of a constructive dismissal claim

An employee may resign (with or without notice) and claim constructive dismissal if the employer has acted in such a way as to fundamentally breach one of the express or implied terms in their contract. The implied duty of care and the implied duty of trust and confidence are two important implied terms that are inherent in every contract of employment (see the section on 'The common law duty of care' in Chapter 1 for a discussion of the implied duty of care).

A breach of the implied duty of trust and confidence can occur either as a result of a single incident (such as an incident of serious bullying or harassment), or as a consequence of a series of actions over a period of time that have combined to destroy trust and confidence in the employment relationship. Essentially, if the level of stress that the employer is causing the employee is wholly unreasonable and has built up to a level where the employee finds the situation intolerable, and so feels that there is no alternative but to resign, a claim for constructive dismissal may succeed. Other examples of breaches of trust and confidence could include:

- bullying or harassment in the course of employment

- a failure on the employer's part to deal adequately with an employee's complaint of bullying or sexual harassment (as was found in the case of *Bracebridge Engineering Ltd v Darby [1990] IRLR*)

- a failure or refusal to deal adequately with an employee's genuine and reasonable complaint about excessive workloads, long hours of work or other workplace pressures that are causing an unacceptable level of stress

- lack of support or training for an employee who has complained that he or she is not coping with a particular aspect of their job

- unfairly or falsely accusing an employee of serious misconduct

- any other behaviour which causes serious stress-related symptoms or which has a serious adverse impact on the employee's morale, self-esteem or self-confidence.

Claims of constructive dismissal are contingent on the employee having a minimum of one year's continuous service with the employer.

How an employer can prevent or reduce the likelihood of employees suffering from workplace stress

It is often said that 'prevention is better than cure'. This maxim could well be applied to workplace stress, as it is clearly in the interests of every employer and employee to prevent a situation arising where people may become ill as a result of stressors at work. The responsibility lies with the employer to identify whatever steps are reasonable and practicable to eliminate the causes of workplace stress and ensure that, wherever possible, employees are not subjected to pressures that could make them ill.

There are many courses of action that an employer can take to minimise the likelihood of employees experiencing excessive levels of stress at work.

Reviewing the job and the way it is done

Often the job itself, or the way the employee is expected to do it, is a source of stress. In order to reduce the likelihood of problems, the employer should:

- make sure every employee has a clearly written job description with clearly defined objectives and is are clear about work priorities

- make sure each employee knows how his or her job fits in with the organisation as a whole and how it interacts with the work of others

- give individuals more control over their day-to-day work whenever possible

- consult employees over work methods with a view to seeking improvements

- take positive steps to cut out any unnecessary work.

Conducting a review of workloads, targets and deadlines

It is often the sheer size of an employee's workload that is the root cause of stress. Instead of imagining that nothing can be done, management should:

- consult employees over workloads, targets and deadlines generally

- consult individuals about how they are coping with their workload

- ensure workloads, targets and deadlines are reasonable

- review whether the demands being made on the employee are within the person's coping resources.

In addition to the above, the employer should:

- recognise the fact that working long hours as a result of a heavy workload can damage the employee's productivity and health

- assess ways of allowing employees who work long hours to reduce their hours, for example by recruiting additional staff, redistributing workloads, restructuring the job, or introducing a rule that imposes a maximum number of working hours on everyone

- make sure all employees take proper breaks and utilise their full holiday entitlement.

These issues are explored more fully in Chapter 3.

Introducing flexible working practices

The topic of flexible working practices is dealt with fully in Chapter 3. In relation to the effective management of stress, however, managers should:

- offer employees a choice, if possible, as to their working pattern and number of hours

- encourage alternative ways of working, such as job-sharing, home working and the introduction of flexible working hours

- encourage employees to achieve a work–life balance.

Ensuring every employee receives sufficient training, support and resources

It is very important to ensure that all employees receive sufficient training, support and resources to enable them to cope with their jobs. Apart from the obvious benefits of providing training, it is important to recognise that the lack of it may cause some employees to feel incompetent and so progressively lose confidence, which in turn can be a great source of stress.

It is particularly important to ensure that appropriate training is provided to an employee who is about to be promoted, transferred to a different job or allocated new responsibilities. The employee's manager should also make time to provide general support and guidance for the first few weeks after the promotion or transfer. This will help the employee to gain confidence and reduce the likelihood of stress during the early period in the new job.

Management should:

- consult individuals about their training needs

- recognise that individuals vary with regard to the amount of training and support they require

- make sure adequate skills training is provided before an employee is promoted or transferred to a different job

- be willing to provide ongoing support whenever it is needed

- consider providing training to employees in stress management, to help them to recognise and deal with stress, both in themselves and in others.

Promoting open, two-way communication

A common complaint from employees in many organisations is lack of communication from management. Where employees are 'kept in the dark' about what is going on within their organisation or not consulted over matters that affect them, then it will not be surprising if they become disgruntled and negative, all of which is likely also to adversely affect their levels of stress. Management should therefore:

- take responsibility for ensuring that communication channels within the organisation are genuinely open at all levels

- take positive steps towards keeping employees fully informed about what is going on within the organisation

- consult employees fully about all matters that might affect them

- provide regular face-to-face feedback to each employee on his or her performance at work, including praise for good work

- provide opportunities for employees to contribute ideas and ensure that when a good idea is put forward, it is properly acknowledged

- encourage employees to bring forward any workplace problems they may have and make sure all employees know they can do so without fear of reprisals

- encourage face-to-face communication wherever possible rather than an explosion of e-mails

- introduce good-practice intranet guidelines to discourage indiscriminate sending of e-mails that risk overloading colleagues with information that is not relevant to their needs

- strive to create a culture that makes it possible for employees who feel stressed at work to come forward and discuss their problems in confidence with their manager

- encourage and organise out-of-work social activities for employees.

Managing change

Change is a part of every organisation's experience, and employees nowadays must learn to cope with many different types of change in the workplace, including business takeovers or mergers, restructuring, the introduction of new methods of work or new managers coming in. Different employees cope in different ways and to different degrees of success with change, and it is well known that many resent and even resist it. Such an attitude is understandable as, when faced with change, most employees will immediately feel anxious about how it will affect them.

The key stressor in times of change is undoubtedly not knowing what will happen or how/when it will happen. Impending changes within the organisation will make employees feel threatened, because everything that is familiar (and therefore comfortable) to them risks being replaced with new, unknown and untried working arrangements. There may be a fear of being unable to cope, or of course a fear of redundancy. It follows that the provision of concrete information to employees in times of impending change will go a long way to reducing the levels of stress that they may otherwise experience.

Management should therefore:

- recognise the damage uncertainty and fear of change can do to individual employees' levels of confidence and wellbeing

- involve employees as much as possible and as early as possible in the plans for change

- talk to employees about how the changes are likely to affect them personally

- provide reassurance wherever possible.

From April 2005 onwards, there will in any event be a legal requirement (as a result of an EU Directive) for employers with 150 or more staff to consult with their employees about matters that affect their employment. This will only be required, however, where a formal request is received from at least 10 per cent of the workforce for an information and consultation forum to be set up. Information and consultation would then have to be about:

- recent and forthcoming developments in the business (i.e. the organisation's performance and strategic planning)

- recent developments concerning the organisation's economic situation

- planned structural changes within the organisation, especially where there is a threat to job security

- decisions likely to lead to substantial changes in work organisation

- any potential changes to terms and conditions of employment.

Consultation in relation to any decisions likely to lead to substantial changes in either work organisation or terms and conditions will have to be carried out with a view to reaching agreement on the decisions to be made.

The statutory duty to inform and consult will be extended to employers with 100 or more staff in April 2007, and finally to employers with 50 or more staff in April 2008.

Implementing anti-bullying/anti-harassment policies

In order to minimise the likelihood of bullying or harassment in the workplace, employers should formulate and implement an anti-bullying/anti-harassment policy and accompanying complaints procedure. Specifically, management should:

- demonstrate a strong commitment to the elimination of bullying and harassment in the workplace

- communicate the policy and complaints procedure fully to all employees

- provide training on harassment awareness and the prevention of bullying and harassment in the workplace

- make it clear that disciplinary action will be taken against any employee who bullies or harasses a colleague, and ensure such disciplinary action is followed through consistently

- always take complaints of bullying or harassment seriously and investigate them promptly and fairly.

The adoption of an anti-bullying policy will help employees to understand that the employer supports their wellbeing and is keen to ensure that the working environment is comfortable for everyone.

The topic of bullying/harassment is dealt with fully in Chapter 4.

Providing an employee assistance programme

One way of helping employees come to terms with workplace stress is to offer an external advice and support service through an independent counselling organisation or qualified specialist provider. This may take the form of a confidential telephone help-line that employees can access free of charge in order to discuss any problems they may be experiencing, or make an appointment with an independent counsellor to discuss their problems face to face. An alternative for larger organisations would be to appoint an appropriate person in-house to fulfil the role of employee welfare officer/counsellor.

If a counsellor is appointed within the organisation, the role could include some or all of the following:

- distributing information to employees about stress, its causes and possible symptoms

- offering confidential guidance or advice to employees who believe they are suffering from stress on an on-request basis

- helping employees to identify and recognise the cause(s) of their stress

- helping employees to identify any reasonable courses of action that they could take to address the problem

- making staff aware of methods of reducing stress levels, such as healthy diet and exercise

- where stress is work-related, talking through with employees how they might go about discussing their problems directly with their managers so that an effective solution can be found

- accompanying employees (if they wish) to meetings with their managers to raise the issue of workplace stress.

While the provision of an employee assistance programme is to be recommended in a general sense, it is no substitute for positive measures designed to tackle the potential causes of stress in the workplace and prevent employees becoming stressed in the first place.

A health and safety policy on stress

Under the Health and Safety at Work Act 1974 s2(1), there is a duty on every employer 'to ensure, so far as is reasonably practicable, the health, safety and welfare at work of all his employees'. The Act covers mental health as well as physical health. Thus, if employees suffer injury to their mental health, the occurrence of which was foreseeable and preventable, then the employer is not operating a 'safe system of work' as required by the Act, nor a working environment that is without risks to health.

Where firms employ five or more workers, they are under a statutory duty to prepare and keep up to date a written statement of their general policy on the health and safety at work of their employees, together with the arrangements for putting the policy into practice. They must also bring the health and safety policy and any revisions to the attention of all employees.

The health and safety policy should specifically identify stress as a workplace hazard and include a statement about how the employer will identify factors in the workplace that may lead to employee stress, and what steps they will take to reduce or resolve those factors. Furthermore, in workplaces where the risk of workplace stress is high, there should arguably be an additional specific policy to deal with it.

A health and safety policy dealing specifically with stress will have several advantages. Such a policy will:

- form the foundation of effective stress management

- make it clear to the workforce that the employer is committed to tackling stress in the workplace

- acknowledge that stress is different in nature from other workplace hazards

- highlight stress as an issue that needs to be controlled in parts of the organisation that may not otherwise be involved in risk assessment and control (see below under 'Carrying out stress risk assessments')

- ensure the subject of stress receives ongoing management attention

- help to provide the employer with a sound defence against any legal claim in the event that a worker develops a stress-related illness.

The above benefits will, of course, depend not only on the formulation of a policy on stress but on its proper implementation!

The main aim of a health and safety policy dealing specifically with stress should be to enable the identification of reasonably foreseeable harm to employees' mental health and to provide strategies for preventing it or reducing its effects. This in turn will help employers to fulfil their general statutory duty to provide a 'safe system of work', as required by the Health and Safety at Work Act 1974 s2(a).

Model policy on workplace stress

The model policy/procedure shown in the box below could be adopted or adapted to suit the employer's needs:

> ### Model policy on workplace stress
>
> It is the policy of this Company that no employee will be placed under pressures in the workplace that are likely to cause him or her an unacceptably high level of stress. This includes a commitment not to subject employees to unreasonably high workloads, nor to require employees to work extremely long hours.
>
> Any employee who believes that a particular aspect of his or her job, or an element in the workplace is causing an unacceptable level of stress should, in the first instance, raise the matter with his or her line manager. The line manager will discuss the matter with the employee with a view to identifying the specific workplace factors that are causing the stress, and wherever possible, taking into account operational requirements, agree appropriate steps to remedy the problem and reduce the stress on the employee to a level that he or she can comfortably cope with.
>
> It is the Company's policy to support employees who in good faith raise concerns related to workplace stress, to treat the matter seriously and deal with it promptly, efficiently and in confidence. No employee will be penalised for making a genuine complaint about workplace stress.
>
> The main aim of this policy is therefore to enable management to address genuine complaints of stress at work, so that appropriate steps may be taken to resolve the problem and prevent the situation from continuing or escalating.

Carrying out stress risk assessments

Under the Management of Health and Safety at Work Regulations 1992 s3, employers are under a duty to conduct risk assessments in order to identify and assess any risks to employees' health and safety, and to determine and put in place appropriate measures to prevent or reduce these risks. This statutory duty incorporates the identification of risks to mental health. Organisations with five or more employees must also record the significant risks to which their employees are exposed.

As part of the process of conducting risk assessments, the employer should aim to identify those jobs that are likely to cause high levels of stress. The risks to the employees' health from stress should then be assessed in the same way as any physical risk present in the workplace, so that controls can be put in place to remove or reduce the risks. A risk assessment may be based on jobs or on work activities, or both, but should also take into account the individual doing the job. As part of the process of conducting a risk assessment, the employer should ensure that adequate arrangements are in place for staff to communicate issues of concern to them.

In some jobs, stress will represent one of the most obvious risks to health and safety; examples include jobs in the emergency services, nursing, social services and any other job in which there is a real risk of physical violence. In addition, it is arguable that any job that consistently involves very heavy workloads, excessive hours or working under tight time deadlines is a high-risk job when viewed from the perspective of risks to the employee's mental health. Stress may also be a hazard on account of the susceptibility of the individual performing the job, for example where individuals have a tendency to put themselves under excessive pressure, or have serious personal problems outside the workplace that affect their general wellbeing and level of resilience to workplace stressors. Essentially, whenever stress is a foreseeable hazard, for whatever reason, the organisation's risk assessment must cover it. Realistically, this will be the case in most jobs.

Useful guidance on how to carry out a risk assessment is available in the HSE (Health and Safety Executive) publication *Five Steps to Risk Assessment*.

How to deal with employees who indicate they are suffering from stress or are showing signs of stress

If, despite measures to prevent workplace stress, an employee nevertheless becomes anxious or stressed as a result of factors in the workplace, the line manager should adopt a supportive stance and, in consultation with the employee, take all practicable steps to change the factors that are causing stress so as to remove or reduce their effects. To start this process, the manager should:

- set up an informal private meeting with the employee

- prepare thoroughly, for example by reviewing any history of the employee's pattern of absence

- seek advice from the Human Resources Department if the organisation has one

- at the meeting, try to identify what is causing the problem through the use of open questioning techniques and active listening

- demonstrate support for the employee and make it clear that the aim of the discussion is to help him or her cope with the work

- review ways of reducing or removing the cause of the stress through joint discussion

- consider whether it may be appropriate to suggest the employee undergoes a medical examination

- seek to reach agreement on specific action points to support the employee

- keep matters confidential

- set a review date so that the employee's health and wellbeing can be monitored.

It is important to take action promptly whenever it comes to the manager's attention that there might be a problem involving workplace stress. Whenever the employee's symptoms of stress start to impinge on job performance, attendance or general wellbeing, the problem becomes a management problem. The employee may feel helpless to deal with the problem, and it follows that the responsibility lies with the manager to initiate action to discuss the matter, with a view to offering support where possible. If nothing is done, the problem is likely to continue and may get worse, which in turn may put the employee at risk of suffering serious damage to his or her health.

It will be important for management not only to offer support to an employee who is suffering from workplace stress, but also to exercise a generous degree of tolerance and sympathy. Unless a sympathetic approach is taken, it is unlikely that the employee will be willing even to discuss the problem, and until the problem is fully discussed, it cannot be resolved. It is up to the employer to make sure that staff feel comfortable with the notion of discussing the subject of stress with their managers, with a view to finding ways of removing or reducing the factors causing it.

Adjusting the job or working conditions

Having conducted an interview with the employee to establish the causes of the stress, it will be essential to reach agreement on measures to reduce it. What measures are appropriate will depend of course on what is causing the stress, but may include:

- reducing the employee's workload

- removing any particular element of the job that is causing high levels of stress, such as the requirement to deal with difficult customers

- changing the employee's method of working

- moving the employee to a different job (whether temporarily or permanently)

- agreeing to part-time working or home-working for a time

- developing a plan that will make sure the employee does not work over-long hours

- providing further training or on-the-job coaching/support

- appointing someone in the organisation to mentor the employee for an agreed period of time

- offering to pay for the employee to undergo external counselling.

Such measures should, of course, be undertaken only with the employee's full agreement.

Dealing with employees whose stress is a result of personal factors outside work

Although, in theory, an employer cannot be liable for a stress-related illness that an employee may suffer as a result of personal factors occurring outside work, such factors are very likely in practice to impact on the employee's ability to work effectively. It is unrealistic to imagine that people who are experiencing severe problems in their private lives can simply leave their problems at home and perform their work to the normal standards. At the very least, a high level of distraction is to be expected. Managers should therefore be prepared to show a reasonable degree of tolerance and sympathy to an employee who is experiencing a serious personal or family-related problem.

Furthermore, someone who is experiencing personal or family difficulties that are causing stress may be less capable than usual of tolerating the stressors inherent in the workplace. For example, an employee who normally copes well with a high workload may experience difficulties coping with that workload while experiencing a serious personal problem. Hence the interaction between stress caused by personal factors and stress caused by work-related factors may become blurred. Working life and home life can pull an individual in different directions, cause conflicts in priorities and put great strain on an individual's professional and personal working relationships.

While no employer can be held liable for a stress-related illness that an employee suffers as a result of factors in their personal life, liability could potentially arise if workplace factors combined with personal factors to 'tip the employee over the edge'. If the employer could reasonably have foreseen that the employee would become ill as a result of personal stress aggravated by workplace factors, and if the employer had done nothing to reduce the aspects of work that were adding to the level of stress experienced by that person, then it is possible that liability could accrue to the employer.

Tackling the dysfunctional response of an employee who cannot cope with normal day-to-day pressures

Once the employer has taken all reasonably practicable steps to make suitable adjustments to the employee's job, methods of working, hours of work and so on in order to reduce stress, the employee's wellbeing and performance should be monitored on an ongoing basis. The purpose of this will be to make sure that the measures adopted are having the desired effect: that is, that the employee is now coping adequately with the job and the day-to-day pressures inherent in the workplace without experiencing unacceptably high levels of stress.

If, however, the measures adopted do not succeed and, for example, the employee still finds after a period of time that he or she is unable to cope effectively with normal day-to-day pressures, the employer may reach the conclusion that this person is inherently unable to deal with the normal day-to-day pressures present in the workplace. In reaching this conclusion, however, the employer should take care not to make assumptions about what constitutes 'normal day-to-day pressures'. As discussed above, it will be the employer's responsibility to take concrete steps to support someone who is suffering from workplace stress by making adjustments to the work or working arrangements before reaching such a conclusion. It would also be advisable to seek to obtain a medical report from a suitably qualified doctor about the employee's ability to cope with work (see Chapter 8 for a discussion on medical advice).

If, however, the employer has already taken such positive measures and the employee, despite the support given, is still unable to perform effectively or meet the reasonable demands of the job, the employer may decide to go through a 'capability procedure' that could, eventually, lead to the legitimate termination of employment.

A 'capability procedure' will be a formal process. To undertake this process, the manager should:

- set up a meeting with the employee to review performance and ability, allowing him or her to be accompanied by a colleague or trade union representative if he or she wishes

- explain (gently!) that the employee's continuing inability to meet the requirements of the job has now become a problem for the organisation, and why it is a problem

- give specific examples of ways in which the employee is failing to meet the required standards

- ask the employee why he or she thinks that the measures adopted have not helped to a satisfactory degree

- consider fully any new or continuing mitigating factors

- restate what duties and standards are expected, and check whether the employee believes that these are reasonable

- specify clearly what improvement is required, and check that the employee believes that this is reasonable

- agree a further reasonable timescale for improvement

- arrange any further training or coaching if appropriate

- seek medical advice, either from an occupational health specialist or (with the employee's written consent) the employee's GP

- consider again whether any adjustments can be made to working arrangements, such as a transfer to alternative or part-time work

- warn that employment is likely to be terminated if the employee continues to fail to meet the required standard

- schedule a follow up meeting to review whether performance has improved satisfactorily

- keep full records.

If, following the application of a fair and reasonable capability procedure, the employee still fails to meet reasonable standards of performance, the employer may ultimately consider dismissal (see next section).

Whether and when dismissal is an option

If, due to a stress-related illness, an employee is incapable of performing the job effectively, and if it is clear from medical evidence that there is little likelihood of him or her recovering sufficiently to resume work in the foreseeable future, this can ultimately give the employer grounds to terminate that person's employment. The reason for dismissal will be lack of 'capability', which is one of five potentially fair reasons for dismissal defined in section 98(2)(a) of the Employment Rights Act 1996. Capability as a reason for dismissal is defined as being 'assessed by reference to skill, aptitude, health or any other physical or mental quality'. This provision applies as much to dismissals on account of incapability arising out of a stress-related illness as to incapability arising out of a physical illness or injury. Clearly employees who are on long-term absence from work as a result of any illness, whether stress-related or not, will be incapable of performing their job.

In order for the dismissal to be fair, however, the employer must also act reasonably in treating the employee's incapability as a sufficient reason to justify dismissal, taking into account all the circumstances of the case. In essence this means that the employer must carry out the dismissal in a way that is reasonable, and in particular must follow a fair and proper procedure. Fair procedure will include informing the employee in writing of the circumstances that might give rise to dismissal, full consultation with the employee, obtaining up-to-date medical evidence and establishing whether there is any alternative to dismissal, for example considering whether he or she is well enough to perform a different job, do part-time work or work from home. Employees also have the statutory right to appeal internally against a decision to dismiss.

There is no prescribed length of time after which it may be fair to dismiss an employee who is absent from work due to illness, but the reasonableness of a dismissal will depend on all the circumstances of the case, including whether the employer has reached a stage where it is no longer reasonable for them to wait any longer for the employee to recover and resume normal working.

Even if an employee's illness has been caused by factors in the workplace, and even in circumstances where the employer may be liable for a claim for personal injury, a dismissal on the grounds of ill health can still be a fair dismissal. The issue of whether or not an employee can succeed in a claim for personal injury is an entirely separate matter.

POINTS TO NOTE

- Stress prevention and control is an essential part of the effective management of people at work.

- Managers need to be constantly alert to the possibility of harmful levels of stress among their employees, and ready to take appropriate remedial action as soon as a potential problem is identified.

- There are many potential causes of stress in the workplace, including heavy workloads, tight deadlines, long working hours, the design of jobs, lack of training or support, fear of change, inadequate communication, management styles, poor working relationships, harassment and environmental factors.

- If harm to an employee's mental health is reasonably foreseeable and the employer does nothing to prevent it, the employer will be guilty of negligence and liable for damages for personal injury in the event that the employee does subsequently become ill.

- An employee may resign (with or without notice) and claim constructive dismissal if the employer has acted in such a way as to fundamentally breach the implied duty of care or the implied duty of trust and confidence.

- Every employer's health and safety policy should specifically identify stress as a workplace hazard and include a statement about how the employer will identify factors in the workplace that may lead to stress and what steps they will take to reduce or resolve those factors.

- Although an employer cannot be liable for stress-related illnesses that employees suffer as a result of personal factors occurring outside work, such factors are very likely in practice to affect an employee's ability to work effectively and should be taken into account.

- If the employer has taken all reasonably practicable measures to reduce an employee's stress levels, but despite this the employee is still unable to perform effectively or meet the reasonable demands of the job, the employer may proceed to go through a 'capability procedure' which could, eventually, lead to the legitimate termination of employment.

- Dismissal on account of incapability arising out of a stress-related illness is potentially fair in law, provided the employer has acted reasonably in treating the employee's incapability as a sufficient reason to justify dismissal and followed fair and lawful procedures.

ACTION POINTS

- Recognise that where pressures of work become excessive in relation to an individual's coping resources, the result may be a level of stress that is likely to cause the employee to become ill.

- Acknowledge the fact that different people have different levels of ability to cope with stress.

- Recognise that stress is not dependent only on the amount of workplace pressure, but will result from an imbalance between the amount of pressure placed on an employee and that individual's personal ability to cope with it.

- Where an employee is exhibiting symptoms of stress, initiate action to discuss the symptoms with a view to offering whatever support is possible and practicable.

- Do not imagine, just because no one has come forward to complain, that the problem of workplace stress does not exist in the workplace.

- Be prepared to take concrete action whenever it comes to management's attention that someone has had absences from work attributable to stress, anxiety or depression, or has complained to management about the harmful effects of workplace stress.

- Recognise that any actions or behaviour that cause an employee serious stress-related symptoms or that have a serious adverse impact on morale, self-esteem or self-confidence may breach the implied duty of trust and confidence, entitling the employee to resign and claim constructive dismissal.

- Regularly review jobs, the way jobs are done, workloads, targets and deadlines in order to eliminate or reduce stress among employees.

- Ensure that no employee is allowed to work excessive hours and consider introducing flexible working practices.

- Take positive steps towards keeping staff fully informed about what is going on within the organisation and consult them fully about all matters that might affect them.

- Encourage employees to bring forward any workplace problems they may have (including problems involving stress) and make sure all employees know they can do so without fear of reprisals.

- Consider offering an external advice and support service through an independent counselling organisation or qualified specialist provider.

- Aim, as part of the process of conducting risk assessments, to identify the jobs that are likely to cause high levels of stress to the job holders so that risks to employees' health from stress can be assessed in the same way as any physical risk present in the workplace and controls put in place to remove or reduce them.

- Adopt a supportive stance to anyone who is suffering from serious stress at work and, in consultation with the employee, take all practicable steps to change the factors that are causing stress so as to remove or reduce their effects.

- Show a reasonable degree of tolerance and sympathy to any employee who is under stress due to personal or family difficulties, and recognise that, realistically, this person may be less capable than usual of tolerating the stressors inherent in their workplace.

- Monitor the wellbeing and performance of an employee after any adjustments have been made to a job or working arrangements in order to make sure that he or she is now coping adequately with the day-to-day pressures inherent in the workplace.

CHAPTER 3

WORKING TIME AND THE ADVANTAGES AND IMPLICATIONS OF FLEXIBLE WORKING PRACTICES

Introduction

The effective management of working time and the promotion of flexible working practices are arguably central to the protection of employees' health and wellbeing. Employees who work excessive hours on a regular basis, whether on the basis of paid overtime or simply on account of perceived pressure to do so, are likely to experience regular fatigue and are therefore unlikely to perform their jobs effectively. From the employer's perspective, when it comes to achieving high levels of productivity and resultant business success, focusing on the quantity of hours rather than the quality of employees' work is likely to produce negative outcomes. By contrast, working to remove the 'long hours culture' and offering employees choices as to their working patterns and number of hours (wherever possible) can result in a highly motivated workforce who have both the energy and the inclination to produce high-quality work, which in turn benefits the organisation. Difficulties in balancing home and working lives can cause employees considerable problems and even high levels of stress. The question of the 'work–life balance' is an important feature of modern living that is causing more and more people to reassess their priorities and to demand changes to their employers' practices, the number of hours they work and the level of demands placed upon them at work.

This chapter focuses on working time, from both a legal and practical perspective, with a view to benefiting both employers and their employees.

An overview of the key provisions of the Working Time Regulations 1998

The Working Time Regulations 1998 were implemented in October 1998 as a result of the EU Working Time Directive. It is important to remember that the Directive was introduced as a health and safety measure with the key aim of imposing minimum health and safety requirements in respect of the organisation of working time.

The Working Time Regulations 1998:

- impose a limit on working hours (an average maximum working week of 48 hours for adult workers)

- require employers to grant workers defined minimum rest periods

- impose limits on night working

- provide for a minimum paid holiday entitlement.

The scope of the Working Time Regulations 1998

The Working Time Regulations 1998 apply to all employers, irrespective of size. Exceptions exist with regard to certain jobs, specifically police officers, armed forces personnel, some mobile transport workers who have their own hours regulations (e.g. heavy goods vehicle drivers) and junior doctors under training who are, at the time of writing, only partially covered by the hours limits contained in the regulations.

It is important to note that the regulations apply not only to employees (those employed directly by the organisation) but to the wider category of worker, that is, to anyone who provides services personally to any employer so long as that employer is not a client or customer. Thus agency temps, home-workers, casual staff and the like are all protected. Furthermore, the regulations apply to part-time workers in the same way as to full-timers.

The 'managing executive exemption'

An exemption was included in the Directive allowing certain categories of worker to be excluded from most of the rights it afforded, with the exception of the right to paid holidays. Often known as the 'managing executive' exemption, this means that certain types of worker are not covered by the hours, rest breaks and night-working provisions of the regulations. Those subject to this exemption are, essentially, those who genuinely have control over the number of hours they work to the extent that they can determine when they work, how many hours they work and when they take breaks.

The scope of the term 'managing executive' is, however, to be interpreted quite narrowly. It will apply only to those workers who genuinely have authority to decide for themselves when and how long to work. Some (but not by any means all) senior managers will fall into this category, as potentially will some sales executives and perhaps home-workers whose working hours are not measured, or where hours of work and rest breaks are pre-determined by the worker rather than the employer.

Employers should take care not to assume that a particular worker would fall into the managing executive category. The person must genuinely have full authority and control over his or her hours of work, or in other words, must be able in practice to make day-to-day decisions about when to work without consulting a more senior person.

It is important to note that the managing executive exemption does not apply to holiday entitlement. Consequently, managing executives do enjoy the statutory right to the minimum four-week holiday entitlement imposed by the regulations (see below under 'Holiday entitlements').

In addition to the basic rules in respect of the managing executives derogation, there was an amendment in 1999 to the section of the regulations that deals with unmeasured working time to the effect that some of a worker's time may be exempted from the normal rules in defined circumstances. Specifically, workers who choose of their own volition to work additional hours beyond the portion of their working time that is pre-determined (for example hours beyond the core hours specified in a contract of employment) need not count those hours in respect of the 48-hour limit and are not required to sign an 'opt-out agreement' in respect of those hours (see below under 'The opt-out provision').

It is important to understand that this does not affect employees who are required by their employer to work additional hours, nor anyone who is paid for overtime, but affects only additional hours that a worker chooses to work on a voluntary basis. The sorts of workers likely to fall within this category are those with no defined hours who can in practice determine when they start and finish work, have latitude to prioritise between tasks and can choose how much time to spend on different activities (typically managers).

Equally important is the fact that this provision does not remove any workers affected by it from the right to limit the core hours they work to a maximum average of 48 hours per week, nor from the entitlement to rest breaks and paid annual leave.

Working hours

The philosophy behind the EU Working Time Directive was that no individual should be made to work excessive hours nor denied proper rest breaks at a risk to their health or safety.

The 48-hour week

The core element of the Working Time Regulations 1998 is that workers have the right to decline to work longer than an average of 48 hours per week and cannot be obliged to do so by their employer. Any term in an employment contract that purports to require an employee to work longer than 48 hours per week (on average) will be unenforceable. The number 48 in this context refers to actual working hours, including all overtime. For 'young workers' (i.e. those aged 16 or 17), there is an absolute limit on working hours of 40 hours per week, or eight hours per day, with no provision for averaging.

Averaging (for adult workers) is calculated in most cases over a 17-week reference period. Unless the employer specifies otherwise, this will be a rolling period, which means that employers must ensure that no employee works more than an average of 48 hours per week during any given 17-week period.

In some cases, however, the reference period is 26 weeks, and in certain defined circumstances it can even be 52 weeks. Such averaging provisions should provide employers with sufficient flexibility to plan and organise their work and ensure workloads are taken care of.

Time spent on call

In *Landeshauptstadt Kiel v Jaeger ECJ IRLR 804*, the European Court of Justice (ECJ) addressed the issue of whether the hours spent by an employee who was required to remain at the workplace while on call should be counted as working time. The case was brought by a hospital doctor who, although required to stay at the hospital where he worked while on call, was permitted to sleep in a room provided by the hospital at times when he was not needed.

The outcome of the case was a ruling that all time spent on call at the workplace must be regarded as working time. The key issue leading to that conclusion was that the employee was required to be at the workplace and to be available immediately if needed for duty. The fact that the employee could sleep during some or all of the on-call period was irrelevant, as was the fact that the employer provided a room for this purpose. Such periods of inactivity could not be regarded as rest breaks.

This landmark decision has major implications for any employer whose employees live in or are otherwise required to be at their workplace while they are on call. It would appear that even periods during which they sleep would have to be counted as working time whenever the possibility exists that they may be called out to work during such periods. Employers should therefore conduct a review of the hours of work and rest breaks of any workers whose jobs require them to live in or who are otherwise required to be at their workplace while they are on call.

Since this case, however, the European Commission has put forward proposals to amend the Working Time Directive. If the proposals are approved, this will mean corresponding changes to the UK Working Time Regulations. One of the proposed changes is that there should be two categories of on-call time: active and inactive on-call time. Active time would count towards the 48-hour week, while inactive time (for example time spent asleep at the workplace while on call) would not. These measures are, however, not yet approved and the *Jaeger* case above is, in the meantime, legally binding.

The effect of the 48-hour week on new employees

Because of the averaging mechanism applicable to employees' working hours, employers should pay heed to the hours worked during the first 17 weeks of an individual's employment. This is because a new employee's working hours can only be averaged over the number of weeks they have actually worked. It will thus not be possible for an employee to exceed 48 hours in their first working week, and during the following weeks, the average hours worked over the actual number of weeks employment to date must never exceed 48. This limitation imposed on the hours of new employees may have a particular impact on employers who employ temporary workers to cover peaks in the workload or to undertake special short-term projects.

Where a worker has more than one job

If a worker has more than one job, any organisation that employs that person should take reasonable steps to ensure that his or her total working hours (taking all jobs into account) do not exceed an average of 48 in total. In effect, this would mean putting in place appropriate measures to require employees to inform their managers if they take up other employment, so that the managers can take appropriate steps to ensure the regulations are complied with.

Alternatively, if employees are likely to exceed an average of 48 hours a week in total, the employer should ask them whether they are willing to sign an opt-out agreement (see next section).

The opt-out provision

There is a great deal of controversy over the so-called 'opt-out provision' in the Working Time Regulations that allows individual workers to volunteer, if they wish, to work more than an average of 48 hours per week. Britain was the only EU member state to take advantage of this derogation, and it is claimed by many that its inclusion has meant that the 48-hour limit on the working week has no force or positive practical impact on employees' health.

In order for the opt-out provision to be effective, the following conditions must be met:

- Any agreement whereby an employee volunteers to work more than an average of 48 hours per week must be in writing.

- An employee who has agreed to work more than an average of 48 hours per week has the right to terminate the agreement at any time by giving notice. The default notice period is seven days, but the employer may set up a longer notice period (up to a maximum of three months) by establishing a collective or workforce agreement to that effect.

- It is not permissible to use a collective or workforce agreement to exclude a group of workers from the 48-hour limit. The right to volunteer to opt out is an individual right.

- Any contractual provision requiring an employee to opt out will be ineffective because the employee will, in any event, retain the right to 'opt back in' again: that is, to terminate the opt-out agreement at any time by giving the required amount of notice.

- Employees are protected against any form of detriment, and against dismissal, on account of refusing to agree to opt out of the 48-hour week.

- The employer must keep up-to-date and accurate records of the names of any workers who have opted out of the 48-hour limit.

Young workers (those aged 16 and 17) are not permitted to opt out of the limits imposed by statute on their working hours.

It is important to note that the opt-out provision applies only to the maximum weekly hours provision, and not to rest periods, night working restrictions or holiday entitlements.

Irrespective of the hours provisions contained in the Working Time Regulations 1998, it is advisable for employers to manage their employees' working hours in such a way that they are restricted to a reasonable level. Even if an individual has signed a statement indicating willingness to work more than 48 hours per week on average, this may not be to the advantage of the employer or the employee except as a strictly temporary measure, for example to cope with a short-term peak in the organisation's workload.

Possible future changes

At the time of writing, the European Commission has conducted a review of the Working Time Directive, including the United Kingdom's use of the opt-out provision, as a result of which proposals have been forward for change. Evidence was available that the opt-out provision was being abused by employers, primarily in the United Kingdom; for example workers were sometimes being pressurised into signing opt-out agreements instead of being given a free choice on the matter.

The European Commission has now issued its proposals for amendments to the Working Time Directive (which in turn will have to be incorporated in the UK Working Time Regulations). The proposals are subject to ratification by the European Parliament and European Council and are thus not yet final. The main proposals are that:

- Employers would only be able to use opt-out agreements if their use had been expressly agreed under a collective agreement.

- Where there was no collective or workforce agreement, individual workers would be able to negotiate individually with the employer.

- Employers would no longer be able to ask new employees to consent to opt out at the same time as they signed their contracts, or during any probationary period.

- Consent to opt out would be valid for a maximum of one year and would then have to be renewed.

- No worker would be able to work longer than 65 hours a week, unless a collective agreement provided otherwise.

- Individuals who opted out would have to record the hours that they worked.

There is also a proposal that all employers would be able, by agreement, to extend the reference period for averaging working hours to 52 weeks, thus giving them more flexibility. It should be stressed, however, that these provisions are, at the time of writing, only proposals and there is unlikely to be any change before 2006 at the earliest.

Rest breaks

The Working Time Regulations 1998 impose a requirement on employers to grant certain minimum rest breaks to their workers. These are:

- a rest break during the working day

- a daily rest period

- a weekly rest period.

Although the right for employees to take rest periods is framed in the legislation as an entitlement rather than something that employers must force upon employees, regularly allowing a workaholic employee to forego rest breaks would probably be detrimental to that employee's health and wellbeing. Such an employee's manager would therefore be well advised to speak to him or her concerned to establish the reason for the failure to take proper breaks, and then seek to agree (or if necessary impose) a working pattern that will ensure that rest breaks are taken regularly.

There is no provision in the Working Time Regulations for rest breaks to be paid, and payment is thus a matter for the employment contract to specify.

There are provisions in the regulations for the rest break provisions to be modified or excluded by collective or workforce agreement (see below under 'Permitted exemptions from the rest period provisions'). In such cases, however, the workers concerned must be granted equivalent periods of leave at an alternative time.

Rest breaks during the working day

If an individual's working day exceeds six hours, he or she must be permitted to take a single break of at least 20 minutes. Workers are entitled, if they wish, to leave their workplace during this rest break.

For young workers, the rest break must be at least 30 minutes where the working day exceeds four and a half hours.

Daily rest period

It is compulsory to grant workers a daily rest period of at least 11 consecutive hours every 24 hours. This refers to the time interval between an employee finishing work one day, and starting work the next day. No averaging is permitted in the application of this provision.

For young workers, the requirement is to grant at least a 12-hour break in any 24-hour period.

Weekly rest period

The regulations impose a compulsory weekly rest period of at least 24 consecutive hours, which may be averaged out over two weeks. This means that it is permissible for employees to work for up to 12 days without a day off, provided they are subsequently permitted to take at least two complete days off, over and above the prescribed daily rest breaks.

Young workers must be granted a weekly rest break consisting of a minimum of 48 consecutive hours (that is, two days off each week). There is no provision for averaging.

Permitted exemptions from the rest period provisions

Certain categories of adult worker (see below) can be exempted from the entitlement to minimum rest periods (and also length of night work). This derogation, however, applies only to rest breaks and night work and has nothing to do with the right for workers to limit their hours to a maximum average of 48 per week.

The derogation works by allowing employers to reach agreement with the workforce that they may be excluded from the right to take the laid-down minimum rest periods on the basis that they will be granted equivalent periods of compensatory rest at another time The practical effect of the derogation is that it provides employers some flexibility over the timing of rest periods for certain categories of workers. It is paramount to bear in mind, however, that under this provision rest breaks can in effect only be postponed, not cancelled altogether.

The range of workers potentially covered by the derogation relating to minimum rest periods is fairly broad, and covers the following:

- workers who have to travel a distance to get to work, for example offshore workers, or those who travel extensively between different work-places as part of their work

- security staff, where there is a requirement for a continuous presence throughout the day and night

- workers involved in a business where 24-hour continuity of service or production is required

- workers involved in peak periods of work (for example, work with seasonal highs such as in tourism or agriculture)

- workers affected by unusual and unforeseeable circumstances, or where there has been an accident.

There are also special rules relating to people who work split shifts at different times of the day or who are changing over from day to night shift (or vice versa).

The period of time over which average hours may be calculated (the reference period) is automatically extended to 26 weeks for the above categories of worker. Additionally, a further derogation may be made by means of a collective or workforce agreement to extend the reference period to 52 weeks, provided this can be justified by objective or technical reasons concerning the organisation of work. This could be to the benefit of employers who require maximum flexibility of hours where, for example, there are considerable peaks and troughs in workloads at different times of year, or where employment contracts were set up on the basis of annualised hours.

Night shift working

The Working Time Regulations, as a health and safety measure, impose limitations on night working. Specifically, the regulations impose a requirement that employees' night shifts must not be more than eight hours per night, averaged over a reference period of 17 weeks. Thus, for example, a shift pattern that stipulated that employees must work four 12-hour shifts per week would be acceptable, provided no overtime was worked. If employees' actual night-time working hours exceed, or are likely to exceed an average of eight hours per night, the employer would have to alter the shift pattern so as to comply with the regulations.

It is important to note that this provision stands independently of the general 48-hour week provision. This means that any individual worker's agreement to opt out of the 48-hour week limitation (see above under 'The opt-out provision') will not entitle the employer to extend that employee's night-time hours beyond the eight-hour nightly average.

Young workers are prevented from working during night-time, subject to certain limited exceptions.

Restrictions on night workers who perform hazardous work

The regulations provide for an absolute eight-hour maximum on night working if the employee's work involves special hazards or severe physical or mental strain. This means in effect that no averaging is allowed in these circumstances.

Night work, will be regarded as involving special hazards or severe physical or mental strain if either a workforce or collective agreement has identified it as such, or a risk assessment carried out under the terms of the Management of Health and Safety at Work Regulations 1992 has classified the work as involving significant risk to the health and safety of the workers.

Definition of 'night-time'

The regulations stipulate that night-time must be a period of at least seven hours, and must cover the period spanning midnight to 5.00 am. The specific seven-hour period can be determined by individual employers by means of a workforce or collective agreement. The default, if no workforce or collective agreement is in place, is 11.00 pm until 6.00 am.

Definition of 'night worker'

Night workers are defined as people who work at least three hours during night-time 'as a normal course' or work 'a certain proportion of their annual working time' during night-time. This can mean that someone who works at least three hours during night-time on a regular basis can be classed as a night worker. In *R v Attorney General for Northern Ireland ex parte Burns, [1999] IRLR 315*, for example, the High Court in Northern Ireland ruled that a worker who spent one week of each three-week cycle working at least three hours during the night was a night worker.

Permitted exemptions from the night working provisions

Certain types of workers can be exempted from the provisions relating to the length of night work. The types of work covered by this exemption and the principles applicable are largely the same as those detailed above under 'Permitted exemptions from the rest period provisions'. Similarly, the period of time over which average night-time hours may be calculated (the reference period) is automatically extended to 26 weeks for these categories of worker, and a further derogation may be made to extend the reference period to 52 weeks if this can be justified by objective or technical reasons concerning the organisation of work.

Night workers' rights to free health checks

Night workers are entitled to a free health assessment before being assigned to night work, and subsequently at regular intervals. An annual health check for night workers would in most cases satisfy this requirement.

The purpose of this health assessment is to make sure that night workers are fit to perform night work. If a health assessment identifies that a worker has a potential health problem that is caused by, or exacerbated by, working at night, the worker would have the right to be transferred to day work as soon as possible. There are no derogations from this provision.

Holiday entitlements

The Working Time Regulations 1998 introduced, for the first time, an entitlement to a minimum period of paid annual leave for all workers, including young workers. The minimum period is four weeks per annum and entitlement accrues from the first day of employment. Part-time workers are entitled to a pro rata amount of statutory annual leave, which should be calculated in proportion to the number of days or hours that the person works in a week.

An employer who wishes to grant employees the minimum period of paid annual leave may choose to class any public holidays granted as part of their workers' annual entitlement, provided of course that paid time off is given on these days.

The regulations imposed two important restrictions with regard to the statutory period of annual leave:

- Statutory annual leave must be taken during the holiday year in which it is accrued.

- No cash substitutes for holiday not taken are allowed, except on termination of employment.

Bearing in mind that the aim of the regulations is to ensure that workers receive a proper break from work from a health and safety perspective, it makes sense to ensure that all employees take their full period of holiday leave each year.

The restrictions on carry-over and payment in lieu only apply, however, to the period of statutory leave imposed by the regulations (four weeks), and it follows that where employers grant annual leave in excess of the statutory minimum, they are free to make their own rules and arrangements regarding carry-over and payment in lieu in relation to the portion of leave which is in excess of the statutory minimum.

A number of special provisions exist in the regulations relating to the timing of holidays, notice periods in respect of holidays, employers' rights to nominate dates for annual leave to be taken, and holiday pay on termination. These provisions give employers certain rights to regulate when workers take their statutory leave and/or to modify their rights by means of a collective or workforce agreement.

Accrual of holiday entitlement during periods of leave

When employees are absent from work on sick leave, maternity leave and the like, their contracts of employment will normally remain in force irrespective of whether they are being paid their normal salary or wage. It follows that statutory annual leave under the Working Time Regulations 1998 continues to accrue during such periods. This principle was confirmed in the case of *Kigass Aero Components Ltd v Brown [2002] IRLR 312*.

Although the *Kigass* case dealt with holiday entitlement during periods of sick leave, the principle would apply equally to periods of maternity, adoption, paternity and parental leave.

Another important case, determined by the ECJ, was *Merino Gómez v Continental Industrias del Caucho ECJ [2004] IRLR 407* (see 'Key case 1' in the box below).

Key case 1

Merino Gómez v Continental Industrias del Caucho ECJ [2004] IRLR 407

The employee in this case claimed the right to receive paid holidays as she had been on maternity leave at the time of her employer's annual shutdown. She asked to be allowed to take a period of holiday leave at a later date, but this was refused. She claimed she was entitled to an equivalent period of paid leave in lieu at a later time.

The ECJ made it clear that statutory annual leave and maternity leave are for entirely different purposes (annual leave is for the protection of health and safety, while maternity leave is to protect the pregnant woman's biological condition during pregnancy and allow bonding with the child). An employee is therefore entitled to take annual leave at a time other than during her maternity leave.

The implications of this decision are that where a woman is on maternity leave during a period when her employer has an annual shutdown for the purpose of holidays, she will be entitled to take an equivalent period of holiday leave at another time. Examples could include compulsory leave around Christmas and even public holidays, if these count as part of the four-week statutory leave period. The employee must be allowed to take the holiday leave either before she commences maternity leave, or after she has returned to work.

Dealing with employees who decline to take their holiday entitlement

The right for employees to take a minimum of four weeks' paid annual holiday is framed in the legislation as an entitlement rather than something which employers are compelled to force upon employees. Technically, this means that, while employers must not prevent employees from taking their statutory annual leave entitlement, they need not force a reluctant employee to take leave if he or she chooses not to. This provision could in practice allow employers to decline to manage employees' annual leave in any meaningful way, and just leave it up to individuals to request leave. Clearly there are some employees who may choose, for a variety of reasons, not to take their full period of leave, or to come in to work during periods that are technically classed as part of their holiday period. Employees may, for example:

- take the view that 'presenteeism' is vital to their chances of success in the organisation

- fear that if they are not seen to be present at the workplace for more than a day or two, they will lose their edge when it comes to any chance of promotion

- worry that taking their full period of annual leave will go against them in the event that their employers make compulsory redundancies

- fear disapproval from their managers if they take what they think managers may perceive as 'too much time off'

- dread taking time off because of the certain knowledge that they will come back to a mountain of work

- be so stressed out that they do not realise that a break from work is essential for their own health (see Chapter 2 for a discussion on workplace stress and its effects).

Taking into account the general principle of promoting employees' health and wellbeing, it is clearly in the everyone's interests for employers to manage annual leave: that is, to put positive measures in place that ensure that all workers take their full entitlement of leave each year. To achieve this, it is recommended that line managers should:

- inform all their employees that they are not only encouraged to take their full period of annual leave, but are expected to do so

- encourage staff to decide when they want to take their holidays and to submit requests for holiday dates as early in the holiday year as possible, in order to make planning the department's work easier

- make clear to employees are any restrictions on the taking of annual leave, such as any periods when leave may not be taken, and the reasons why

- set a good example by taking holidays themselves

- halfway through the holiday year, remind all staff who have not either taken or booked holidays that they must make their holiday arrangements within a set further period (for example by stipulating that all holiday arrangements must be settled within the next month)

- at a point approximately two-thirds of the way through the holiday year, warn staff who have not yet arranged all their holiday dates that they must do so with the next month, and that if they do not do so, the manager will nominate dates on their behalf

- follow through on the above point by notifying those employees who have still failed to arrange their holidays of set dates on which they will be compelled to take the outstanding portion of their annual holiday entitlement (this is permitted under Regulation 15 of the Working Time Regulations 1998).

When nominating holiday dates for an employee, the employer must give written notice of the dates to be taken equivalent to at least twice the length of the period of leave that they require the employee to take. So, for example, where the employer wished to require an employee to take two weeks annual leave on nominated dates, four weeks notice would be required.

Promoting a work–life balance and discouraging a long-hours culture

Many people nowadays need to combine work with family responsibilities, and consequently need to achieve a sensible and satisfactory balance between the two. The issue of work–life balance is not only relevant to women. The traditional model of working life whereby the man in the family works full time and the woman stays at home to look after the children is long gone. Many families have commitments and lifestyles that mean both adults in the family have to work to make ends meet, and it follows logically that both may wish to share in childcare, elder-care and domestic responsibilities. In addition, it is perfectly reasonable for every person to want to have sufficient free time to pursue a hobby, undertake a part-time course of study, enjoy sport and exercise and follow personal interests outside of work.

Furthermore, research carried out in recent years consistently shows that many employees are disillusioned with the number of hours they are expected to work and would welcome a change to a more flexible approach where the desire to enjoy a personal life outside of work was respected.

The advantages of promoting a work–life balance

The benefits to employers of promoting a work–life balance may be difficult to measure, but doubting employers should perhaps consider also the effects of not allowing their workers to balance their working life with their private and family lives (see next section).

Some of the benefits of promoting a work–life balance can be that:

- Employees are likely to demonstrate more loyalty and commitment to the employer if the employer is showing consideration for their needs.

- Increased loyalty and commitment lead to better performance at an individual level, and thus increased productivity at an organisational level.

- There will be a decrease in sickness absence and its associated costs.

- There will be a lower staff turnover, substantially reducing the employer's recruitment, induction and training costs.

- A more relaxed and flexible workplace culture can encourage employees to come forward with ideas and suggestions for improvement, which in turn can benefit the organisation.

- The employer will become an employer of choice and will be more able to attract and retain the best people.

The practical and legal effects of condoning a long-hours culture

Employers who want to get the most out of their workers should seriously consider the potentially negative consequences of allowing, encouraging or condoning workaholic habits in their employees. Whatever the motive behind long working hours, the employee who regularly works them is unlikely to be as productive as someone who has a reasonable balance between working life and personal life.

Britain has the longest working hours in Europe and many employers still place emphasis on the quantity of hours that employees work, rather than output or the quality of work. This attitude encourages 'presenteeism', the notion that an employee must be seen to be at work for as many hours as possible in order to be viewed as committed to the job. The result is that many employees struggle, and often fail, to juggle long working hours with family responsibilities. It is well established that employees who work more hours do not necessarily produce more work, or higher-quality work, and in many cases the exact opposite may occur.

Some of the specific negative consequences of condoning a long-hours culture and not encouraging a work–life balance can be that employees:

- become exhausted, demotivated and dissatisfied

- produce less work and/or lower quality work

- develop an array of minor ailments and become more prone to illness, thus increasing the likelihood of sickness absence, which can become a major cost to the business

- feel guilty if they do not work long hours and thus become distracted and disillusioned

- develop symptoms of workplace stress, possibly leading to serious ill-health, which in extreme cases could result in legal claims against the organisation (see Chapter 2)

- do not have enough time to spend with their partners and/or children, with the result that their personal relationships (and consequent sense of wellbeing) suffer

- feel forced into making an unfair and unrealistic choice between demonstrating dedication to their job through presenteeism and giving a reasonable amount of time and commitment to their family

- believe that they will be perceived as lacking in commitment if they ask for time off, or that they will forfeit any realistic chance of advancement at work if they dare to break out of the mould and maintain a reasonable balance between working hours and family responsibilities

- are unlikely to feel loyalty and dedication to their employer in the long term

- eventually become fed up and resign, which represents a loss of valuable talent and potential for the employer, and creates significant extra recruitment costs.

Why a requirement for long hours often discriminates against women

Where an employer operates a system (whether formal or informal) under which employees are required or expected to work long hours, unsocial hours (e.g. night-shift working) or even full-time hours, these arrangements will have a disproportionate adverse impact on female employees. There has been a long line of court and tribunal decisions that have upheld the general principle that fewer women than men can comply with a requirement to work long hours due to child-care responsibilities, and that women are therefore more likely than men to be disadvantaged by such practices. This means in effect that women required to work such hours may be able to succeed in a claim for indirect sex discrimination at an employment tribunal unless the employer can justify the practice in question.

To justify to a tribunal a requirement for long hours or a demand that a female employee with children should work full-time, the employer would have to show that the working pattern in question was, on the balance of probabilities, appropriate and necessary for the effective performance of the job.

Examples of working-time patterns that could be indirectly discriminatory against women include:

- a regular requirement for overtime

- compulsory weekend working

- an early start or a late finish

- occasional or regular night working

- shift working, especially if the shift-pattern involves irregular hours or rotating shifts.

Key case 2

In *Chief Constable of Avon and Somerset Constabulary v Chew EAT [2001] (503/00)*, a female police officer succeeded in a claim for indirect sex discrimination when her employer insisted that she should work shift rosters in order to be entitled to work part-time. The employee, who had two pre-school-age children, had recently separated from her husband, and wished to work part-time on day shifts only.

The employment appeals tribunal (EAT) reviewed the well-established principle that a requirement to work shifts or unsocial hours will have a disproportionate adverse impact on women as compared with men. The issue was not whether the police force could justify shift working in a general sense, but rather whether it was justifiable for them to apply the requirement for shift work to the police officer in question under all the relevant circumstances. The evidence suggested that at the relevant time, other posts involving regular day-shift working were available. The EAT thus held that the police force's insistence that the police officer must work the shift patterns in order to be granted part-time work was not justifiable.

This does not mean that an employer can never impose requirements for staff to work long hours or shift patterns. The important point to remember is that any requirement imposed on an employee must be justifiable in terms of the needs of the job. This in reality breaks down into two elements:

1. Whether it is justifiable in a general sense for the employer to operate a policy or practice of requiring employees to work long hours or shift rotas.

2. Whether it is justifiable to apply such a policy or requirement to the individual employee in question when all the circumstances are considered (which will depend in part on what, if any, other options are reasonably available).

It is advisable therefore when reviewing any practice of working long hours to:

- consider carefully the effect that such an arrangement might have on employees, both generally and individually

- adopt a positive approach towards any employee who has difficulty complying with a requirement to work long hours

- endeavour either to adapt the policy or requirement to accommodate such an employee or to exempt the employee from the requirement

- seek to take specific steps to remove the need for employees to work long hours permanently.

It is important to bear in mind that any demand for employees to work long hours that cannot be objectively justified is likely to amount to indirect sex discrimination against any female employee who is disadvantaged by it.

Management's responsibility to change the long-hours culture

Employers who wish to protect and promote their employees' health and wellbeing and ensure the smooth running of their business should:

- respect employees' rights to restrict their working hours under the Working Time Regulations 1998

- encourage employees to restrict their working hours to a reasonable level and take positive action to reduce the hours of any employee who has workaholic tendencies

- ensure, through effective planning, that employees take proper rest breaks and their full annual holiday entitlements

- manage their employees in a realistic way, understanding that expecting them to produce competent work when they are working intolerably long hours is counterproductive

- respect the wishes of employees to achieve a fair and reasonable balance between their working lives and their home lives

- adopt a positive approach towards introducing alternative working patterns.

If a long-hours culture exists, the employer should:

- establish top management commitment to change the culture so as to promote employees' health and wellbeing, which in turn will benefit the business

- carry out a review of employees' views and attitudes to working time and work–life balance, perhaps by conducting a confidential attitude survey and thoroughly analysing the results

- seek to identify and assess specific ways of allowing employees who work long hours to reduce their hours, for example by recruiting additional staff, redistributing workloads or re-structuring operations

- consider and promote alternative ways of working wherever possible, for example job-sharing, term-time working or the introduction of flexitime (see next section)

- consult employees about the options for alternative ways of working

- devise procedures under which employees can raise matters associated with working hours and the work–life balance for discussion with an appropriate person, with a view to making adjustments where possible.

Flexible working practices

Adopting flexible working policies and practices essentially means giving workers a choice, within reason, with regard to their working pattern: the number of hours they work and the days and times when they work. It is about seeking to achieve a reasonable balance so that the needs of individual employees can be met while ensuring that the efficiency and success of the business is maintained at a high level. It is also about being open-minded and willing to change traditional methods of working, and even the culture of the organisation, if working long hours is the norm. Promoting flexible working practices will benefit both employers and staff in terms of increased motivation and loyalty to the business, and more energy and enthusiasm directed by employees into their work.

No single working pattern is suitable for all employees, or for all organisations. For example, working in the evenings and/or at weekends might fit in with some people's needs, while for others, work at these times would be difficult, inconvenient or even impossible.

Types of flexible working

There are many different types of flexible working patterns, including:

- part-time work, which itself can take many forms such as working mornings or afternoons only, working school hours, working alternate weeks or working full-time hours on only two or three days per week

- job sharing, where one job is divided up so that it can be performed by two (or more) individuals, each of whom works part time

- term-time working, which means a contract (whether full or part-time) requiring the employee to work only during the term times of the school year

- compressed hours, for example working three or four long days each week rather than five 'normal' days, or working a nine-day fortnight

- annualised hours, a pattern of work that involves the employee working an agreed number of hours over the year, but with no set pattern or number of weekly hours

- a system of flexitime, an arrangement whereby employees are required to work a pre-defined number of hours over a reference period (usually a month) but can choose, within set limits, the times they start and finish work on different days

- working from home for all or part of the employee's working hours.

The general implications of offering flexible working

Flexibility in working practices provides a valuable benefit to employees, and allows them to maintain a reasonable balance between working time and their family responsibilities and personal lives. Often the flexibility that an employee wants will require only a minor adjustment to standard working practices; for example, an employee who is a single parent may wish to start work half an hour later in the morning in order to be able to take a child to school, and then take a shorter lunch break to make up the time.

Adopting a flexible approach to working practices can offer the employer considerable benefits in terms of employee morale and motivation. Conversely, refusing to grant simple requests to make marginal changes to an employee's working hours may result in the employer losing competent staff who will choose to take their skills and expertise elsewhere, to an employer who is prepared to operate more lifestyle-friendly policies and practices.

The right for employees who have children under six to request flexible working

Following implementation in April 2003 of the Flexible Working (Procedural Requirements) Regulations 2002 and the Flexible Working (Eligibility, Complaints and Remedies) Regulations 2002, an employee who has a minimum of six months continuous service (but not other workers) and who has (or whose partner has) a child under the age of six may submit a formal written request for flexible working to his or her employer. If an employee has a disabled child, a request may be submitted up until the child's 18th birthday. Both men and women are eligible.

Irrespective of the statutory provisions, employers may prefer to extend such a policy to all employees, and not just those who are the parents or carers of children under the age of six.

At the time of writing, there is a proposal to extend the right to request flexible working to employees who have caring responsibilities for elderly or disabled relatives.

The right to request flexible working includes the right for employees to request changes to:

- the number of hours they work

- the times they work (i.e. the days worked and start/finish times)

- the place of work (i.e. employees submit a request to do some or all of their work from home).

An employer who receives a request for flexible working is not obliged to agree to it automatically but must (if the request is not agreed at the outset) follow through a defined procedure that includes holding a meeting with the employee within 28 days in order to explore how the idea might be made to work.

If a request for flexible working is refused, there must be a valid business reason for the refusal and the employee must be told in writing why it applies to this specific case. The employee also has the statutory right to appeal internally if the request is refused. Valid reasons contained within the legislation are:

- the burden of additional costs

- a detrimental effect on ability to meet customer demand

- a detrimental effect on quality

- a detrimental effect on performance

- inability to reorganise work among existing staff

- inability to recruit additional staff

- insufficient work during the periods the employee wishes to work

- planned structural changes.

This represents an exhaustive list and employers are not entitled to invent their own reasons for refusing an employee's request for flexible working, whatever the circumstances.

Under the Part-Time Workers (Prevention of Less Favourable Treatment) Regulations 2000, where a switch from full-time to part-time working is agreed, the employee will have the right to terms and conditions under the new part-time contract that are no less favourable (on a pro rata basis) that those that applied under the previous full-time contract. This means, for example, that an employer cannot require an employee to accept a lower rate of pay if he or she wants to move to part-time working in the same job.

Check-list for the effective management of requests for flexible working

- Put procedures in place to deal with requests, and decide who will be responsible for dealing with them and who will hear any appeals.

- Consider extending the right to request flexible working to all staff, and not just those who are the parents or carers of children under the age of six.

- Train line managers to deal with requests.

- Communicate the right to request flexible working to employees through the appropriate channels, for example staff handbooks.

- Where an employee is on maternity leave, keep in touch with her to establish whether she might wish to switch to part-time working on her return to work, and if so, encourage her to make the request early.

On receipt of a request for flexible working, managers should:

- Check that the employee is eligible (i.e. that they are the parent or carer of a child under six and have at least six months service).

- Ensure a meeting is arranged within the prescribed timescale (28 days).

- Encourage the employee to suggest more than one alternative pattern of working.

- Encourage the employee (at the meeting) to offer suggestions based on his or her experience as to how the desired working pattern could be made to work (for example, how a job could be divided up so as to facilitate a job-share arrangement).

- Be prepared to consider the request with an open-minded attitude, irrespective of the type of work or level of seniority applicable to the job.

- If in doubt, agree a trial period, and ensure the agreement to take this course of action is properly documented.

- Before refusing the request, be certain there is a proper reason to refuse, and clear evidence to support the reason for the refusal: in other words, that there really is no alternative but to refuse the request.

- Agree variations to the employee's contractual terms in writing.

The right of part-time workers not to suffer discrimination on grounds of their part-time status

Under the Part-Time Workers (Prevention of Less Favourable Treatment) Regulations 2000, part-time workers are protected against all forms of discriminatory treatment on the grounds of their part-time status, unless the treatment can be justified in the particular circumstances. The regulations cover pay, terms and conditions of employment, access to and benefits from occupational pension schemes, and non-contractual issues such as training, appraisal and opportunities for promotion and transfer.

Although the Part-Time Workers Regulations do not confer a right for employees to switch from full-time to part-time working, courts' and tribunals' interpretation of sex discrimination legislation has led to the principle that a refusal to allow a woman with caring responsibilities to reduce her hours may amount to indirect sex discrimination (see above under 'Why a requirement for long hours often discriminates against women').

Model policy on part-time working

Employers may wish to adopt a policy on part-time working along the lines shown in the box below.

Model policy on part-time working

It is the policy of this Company that all part-time employees will be treated as valued and committed members of staff, irrespective of the number of hours they work per week or per month. The principle of equality will be applied to part-time employee's pay, contractual terms and non-contractual benefits, which will be offered to part-timers on an equivalent (pro rata) basis to that which is available to comparable full-time staff. The Company will also ensure that opportunities for training and access to promotion are made available on an equal basis to full-time and part-time employees wherever possible.

Access to the Company's pension scheme is open to all employees, irrespective of the number of hours they work, and benefits available under the scheme are equivalent (on a pro rata basis) for both full-time and part-time employees. Entry to the Company's pension scheme is, however, dependent on the employee having gained a minimum of [x months] length of service.

It is the policy of this Company that no employee will be disadvantaged or afforded less favourable treatment of any kind on the grounds of the number of hours they work per week or per month.

POINTS TO NOTE

- The work–life balance is an important feature of modern living that is causing more and more people to reassess their priorities and demand changes to their employers' practices, the number of hours they work and the level of demands placed upon them at work.

- The Working Time Directive, which requires employers to allow workers to limit their working hours to a maximum average of 48 hours per week, take defined minimum rest periods, restrict night working hours and be granted four weeks paid holiday entitlement, was introduced as a health and safety measure.

- Although individual employees may volunteer to opt-out of the 48 hour week (i.e. work longer than 48 hours per week on average), employers may not coerce or oblige them to do so.

- The Working Time Regulations 1998 impose a requirement on employers to grant their workers a rest break during the working day of at least 20 minutes, a daily rest period of 11 consecutive hours and a weekly rest period equivalent to one day off per week.

- Although there is a derogation from the rest break provisions available in respect of certain jobs, employers must always grant equivalent periods of compensatory rest to workers who have not been granted rest breaks at the original time.

- Under the Working Time Regulations 1998, workers' night shifts must not be more than eight hours per night, averaged over a reference period of 17 weeks, and an absolute eight hour maximum is imposed where the employee's work involves special hazards or severe physical or mental strain.

- Many people have to combine work with family responsibilities, and consequently need to achieve a sensible and satisfactory balance between the two.

- There are many benefits to employers of promoting a work–life balance and flexible working practices, and many potential negative consequences for employers who condone a long-hours culture.

- Adopting flexible working policies and practices essentially means giving workers a choice, within reason, with regard to their working pattern, that is, the number of working hours and the days and times when they work.

- Promoting flexible working practices will benefit both employers and employees in terms of increased motivation and loyalty to the business, and more energy and enthusiasm directed by employees into their work.

- Any employee who has a minimum of six months continuous service and who has a child under the age of six (or whose partner has a child under six) has the statutory right to request flexible working, and the employer is required to follow through a defined procedure to consider the request.

- Part-time workers are protected against all forms of discriminatory treatment on the grounds of their part-time status.

ACTION POINTS

- Respect the right of all workers to choose not to work longer than an average of 48 hours per week.

- Review the hours of work, rest breaks and on-call requirements of any workers whose jobs require them to live in or who are otherwise required to be at their workplace while they are on call.

- Take reasonable steps, where someone has a second job, to ensure that either the employee's total working hours (taking both jobs into account) do not exceed an average of 48 in total, or that he or she has voluntarily signed an opt-out agreement.

- Manage employees' working hours in such a way that they are restricted to a reasonable level, and recognise that even if an individual has agreed to opt out of the 48 hours limitation, this may not be to the advantage of the employer or the employee.

- Speak to any employee who is in the habit of not taking his or her full rest breaks to establish the reason for this and then agree (or if necessary impose) a working pattern that will ensure that rest breaks are regularly taken.

- Ensure all night workers receive a free health assessment before being assigned to night work, and are subsequently checked at regular intervals.

- Respect all workers' rights to take their full period of annual holiday leave and to continue to accrue annual leave while on sickness absence or maternity leave.

- Put positive measures in place to manage annual leave so as to ensure that all workers take their full entitlement of annual leave each year.

- Understand that, unless it can be objectively justified, any demand for employees to work long hours will be likely to amount to indirect sex discrimination against any female employee who is disadvantaged by it.

- Consider carefully the negative effect that long hours might have on employees, both generally and individually, and adopt a positive approach towards any employee who has difficulty complying with a requirement to work the hours required by his or her job.

- Respect the wishes of employees to achieve a fair and reasonable balance between their working lives and their home lives.

- Carry out a review of employees' views and attitudes to working time and the work–life balance, perhaps by conducting a confidential attitude survey.

- Seek to identify and assess specific ways of allowing employees who work long hours to reduce their hours, for example by recruiting additional staff, redistributing workloads or re-structuring operations.

- Consider and promote alternative ways of working wherever possible, for example job-sharing, term-time working or the introduction of flexitime.

- Consider extending the right to request flexible working to all staff, and not just those who are the parents or carers of children under the age of six.

- Be prepared to consider requests for flexible working with an open-minded attitude, irrespective of the type of work or level of seniority applicable to the job.

HARASSMENT AND BULLYING

Introduction

Bullying or harassment at work is an issue that the management in every organisation should take very seriously, as its negative effects can be significant. For example it can lead to:

- a general atmosphere of intimidation and fear

- severe stress for the employee being bullied or harassed, leading potentially to long-term ill-health

- low morale and consequent low productivity

- poor working relationships

- increasing levels of absenteeism

- high turnover of competent staff

- legal claims against the employer.

Employees who are being bullied or harassed are unlikely to be able to concentrate fully on their work, and both performance and productivity are therefore likely to suffer. Health problems can develop such as depression or anxiety, which in turn can lead to high levels of both short and long-term absenteeism. Employers who wish to promote their employees' health and wellbeing will need therefore to devise and implement procedures and practices that operate to prevent bullying and harassment in the workplace. They will also need to ensure that any instances of bullying that do occur are addressed decisively.

It is important for employers to be vigilant to the possibility of bullying and harassment in the workplace. Given that research shows clearly that the problem of bullying at work is widespread, it should never be assumed that, just because no one has complained, the problem does not exist within the organisation. Many employees are afraid to complain, especially if the person bullying them is their line manager or immediate supervisor. Alternatively, they may fear retaliation if they complain, or simply feel too embarrassed or distressed to speak out. Some forms of bullying are so underhand and subtle that they may leave the victims feeling that perhaps they are to blame.

This chapter deals with harassment and bullying in the employment context and aims to provide an understanding of how employment laws impact on this area, the steps employers should take to prevent harassment and bullying, and how they should deal with any complaints that may arise despite preventative measures.

Harassment as a form of unlawful discrimination

The law governing harassment at work has developed substantially in recent years, both as a result of court and tribunal decisions that have interpreted harassment as a detriment under discrimination law, and as a result of new legislation which has, for the first time, provided a statutory definition of harassment.

As a result of these developments, harassment on grounds of sex, trans-gender status, race, religion or belief, sexual orientation or disability is regarded in law as a form of unlawful discrimination, giving the victim the right to bring a case to an employment tribunal.

Most of Britain's anti-discrimination laws contain a statutory definition of harassment. The one exception is the Sex Discrimination Act (SDA) 1975, although it is set to be amended in October 2005 to include statutory definitions of both sexual harassment and sex-based harassment. The absence of a statutory definition in the SDA to date has not, however, hindered courts and tribunals from finding that sexual harassment at work is a form of unlawful direct discrimination whenever the behaviour complained of is of a sexual nature and is unwelcome and offensive to the person on the receiving end.

Where harassment is related to race, religion or belief, sexual orientation or disability, there is a statutory definition in the relevant legislation making it a distinct form of unlawful discrimination. The Race Relations Act 1976, for example, states that:

> A person subjects another to harassment where, on the grounds of that other's race or ethnic or national origins, he engages in unwanted conduct which has the purpose or effect of –
>
> (a) violating that other's dignity, or
> (b) creating an intimidating, hostile, degrading, humiliating or offensive environment for that other.
>
> Conduct shall be regarded as having the effect specified in paragraphs (a) and (b) if, and only if, having regard to all the circumstances, including, in particular, the perception of that other, it should reasonably be considered as having that effect.

Interpretation of harassment

Thus harassment has been introduced to statutory law as a free-standing ground of unlawful discrimination, with the proviso that treatment that has an alleged discriminatory effect must also be capable of being interpreted as harassment by a reasonable person.

The 'reasonable bystander test', as it is sometimes known, provides an objective dimension and a yardstick of reasonableness for judging whether or not conduct that has had an alleged detrimental effect on the person experiencing it amounts to unlawful harassment. The person's subjective perception of the alleged harassment stands to be balanced against an objective, reasonable viewpoint, taking into account all the circumstances of the particular case.

For example, if an over-sensitive black African employee unreasonably took offence at a one-off innocent remark about black people that most reasonable people would not have perceived as offensive in the circumstances in which it was made, then a complaint to a tribunal alleging unlawful racial harassment would be unlikely to succeed. In contrast, if racist remarks were regularly being made in the workplace and these caused genuine offence to a black employee, then the employee would potentially be able to succeed in a claim for racial harassment regardless of whether his or her white colleagues found the remarks amusing. The difference is that any banter that is racist in nature is likely to be viewed as potentially offensive by most reasonable people. Furthermore, it has been established for some time as a result of court and tribunal decisions that it is for each individual to determine individually what they find offensive.

An interesting element of the definition of harassment is the concept that a complaint of harassment can be brought on the grounds that an employee finds a working environment intimidating, hostile, degrading, humiliating or offensive. One consequence of this approach is that it is possible for individuals to claim unlawful harassment even where the conduct complained of is not directed at them personally. For example, if managers condone an atmosphere at work in which it is common for employees to engage in homophobic banter, then this might be said to have created an offensive working environment for an employee who is gay, irrespective of whether any of the banter was directed at that particular person.

What constitutes harassment?

The principle that employees are entitled to decide for themselves what conduct they perceive as unwanted and offensive is a key element in anti-discrimination law. It is important to recognise that people differ, and what one person finds funny or harmless may be offensive or embarrassing to someone else. This principle is enshrined in the EC Code of Practice on the protection of the dignity of women and men at work, which states that:

- Sexual harassment is 'unwanted conduct of a sexual nature, or other conduct based on sex affecting the dignity of women and men at work'.

- Conduct of a sexual nature will amount to sexual harassment where it is 'unwanted, unreasonable and offensive to the recipient'.

- It is for each individual to determine what behaviour is acceptable to him or her and what is offensive.

It can be seen from the EU's approach to sexual harassment (which has been observed and upheld for many years by UK courts and tribunals) that the decision as to whether particular conduct amounts to sexual harassment lies with the victim. It follows that managers responsible for staff should take care not to view behaviour purely subjectively, as this may lead them to view an allegation of sexual harassment as insignificant in circumstances where the recipient of the behaviour has been genuinely offended. The important criterion is whether the recipient of the conduct finds it offensive, and not whether the manager regards it as trivial, or as a joke. The same principles would apply to harassment on grounds of race, religion or belief, sexual orientation and disability.

A complaint of unlawful harassment can be taken to tribunal as a result of either a single serious incident of harassment or a series of relatively minor incidents that, when viewed collectively, can be classed as a campaign of conduct amounting to unlawful harassment or causing detriment to the victim. The EAT held for example in *Driskel v Peninsula Business Services Ltd & ors [2000] IRLR 151* that a series of verbal incidents may become a discriminatory detriment if persisted in, irrespective of whether the employee expressed an objection at the time the remarks were made. In the same case, the EAT held that an employer will not be able to defend a claim for sexual harassment on the basis that vulgar comments and sexual remarks were made equally to both men and women. The tribunal took the view that, even though both sexes were subjected to the same remarks, women were likely to find the remarks more intimidating than men, and hence the effect of the remarks was to place women at a disadvantage as compared to men.

Different forms of harassment

Harassment may occur for many reasons. It may have many underlying motives, or in some cases no motive at all, and its effects on different people will vary. It may be deliberate, or unintentional. It may be directed at a particular individual, or may consist of remarks or jokes told to a group of people with no specific target. Its effects may range from mild discomfort to extreme distress. Whatever its motive, form or effect, two things are certain: harassment of any kind is completely unacceptable in modern workplaces and it may give rise to legal claims against the employer for unlawful discrimination.

Many types of conduct will be capable of being interpreted as unlawful harassment if the conduct is related to sex, trans-gender status, marital status, sexual orientation, race, religion or belief, or disability (and – after October 2006 – age), provided the conduct in question had the effect of making the victim feel distressed in some way or created a working environment in which the employee felt uncomfortable.

Sexual harassment

In *Strathclyde Regional Council v Porcelli [1986] IRLR 134,* the first case of its kind, the Scottish Court of Session ruled that sexual harassment need not be based on a sex-related motive for it to constitute unlawful discrimination. Provided the unfavourable treatment to which a woman was subjected included a significant sexual element to which a man would not be vulnerable, then it would be regarded as direct sex discrimination. Of course this principle could apply the other way around, as men can also be the victims of sexual harassment.

The EC Code of Practice on the protection of the dignity of women and men at work points out that sexual harassment can consist of physical, verbal or non-verbal conduct (see below under 'Physical, verbal and non-verbal harassment').

Harassment on grounds of sexual orientation

The implementation of the Employment Equality (Sexual Orientation) Regulations 2003 in December 2003 made it unlawful to harass someone at work on grounds that the person is, or is thought to be, gay, lesbian or bi-sexual (or heterosexual). Harassment may take many forms, but often consists of derogatory or insulting remarks directed towards a gay man or lesbian woman.

Racial harassment

The Race Relations Act 1976 prohibits discrimination and harassment on grounds of colour, race, nationality and ethnic or national origins. 'National origins' in this context has been ruled to include the distinction between the English and the Scots. Thus the Act is very wide in its scope. Forms of harassment may include:

- calling someone a nickname linked to nationality or skin colour

- making derogatory remarks that are clearly linked to a person's ethnic background

- racial innuendoes or offensive language related to racial or ethnic origins

- racist jokes or banter.

Harassment on grounds of religion or belief

Since the implementation of the Employment Equality (Religion or Belief) Regulations 2003 in December 2003, employees are expressly protected against any harassment on grounds of their religion or belief. 'Religion' is defined broadly as 'any religion, religious belief or similar philosophical belief'. The regulations have immense implications for employers. Different forms of harassment might include:

- teasing, taunting or ridiculing colleagues because of their religious views, any mode of dress linked to their religious beliefs, or customs (such as praying during the working day)

- overt allegiances (for example wearing a t-shirt displaying a football slogan that has a sectarian significance) to football clubs that are linked to sectarian groups, for example the rivalry between Rangers and Celtic supporters in Glasgow

- preaching religious beliefs at length to colleagues with the aim of 'converting' them, which might be viewed as offensive.

Harassment on grounds of disability

The principles of harassment apply equally to behaviour linked in some way with an individual's disability, whether physical or mental. Forms of harassment may include:

- innuendoes, banter or jokes about people with disabilities generally

- using insulting terminology or name-calling

- ridiculing someone on account of a disability

- excessive staring

- mimicking a disabled employee's mannerisms or speech.

Physical, verbal and non-verbal harassment

Harassment may be physical, verbal or non-verbal.

Physical harassment

Physical harassment is most likely to occur in the form of sexual harassment: for example fondling, patting, or any type of unwelcome touching with a sexual connotation. This does not mean of course that every instance of physical contact amounts to harassment; a friendly pat on the arm, for example, may be entirely innocent. Nevertheless, if a particular individual finds such behaviour unacceptable, he or she would have the right to say so and ask the person to desist. Then, if the patting continued despite the clear intimation that it was unwelcome or unacceptable, there might be an argument that such further instances of behaviour to which the person had clearly objected did constitute harassment.

Verbal harassment

Verbal harassment at work is far more common than physical harassment. It may include (for example):

- language that is of a sexual nature or racially offensive

- sexist or racist remarks made to or about an employee

- general banter in the workplace that might be linked (for example) to race, religion or sexual orientation

- e-mails containing vulgar jokes or jokes with a sexual connotation that might cause offence or embarrassment

- calling someone by a name based on sex, race or sexual orientation, for example calling a female colleague 'blondie' (which could be perceived as demeaning on account of the dumb-blonde stereotype) or an Asian employee 'Paki' (which was expressly ruled by a Court in 2003 to be racially offensive), or referring to a lesbian colleague as 'lezzie' (which she might regard as insulting)

- making derogatory remarks or using offensive terminology linked to race, religion, gender, sexual orientation or disability; for example using the term 'wog' when referring to a black employee or 'cripple' when describing a disabled person

- teasing directed at an employee on account of the fact he or she has a same-sex partner or a close relative or friend who is gay or lesbian

- teasing on the subject of religious convictions or religious practices

- persistent sexual advances or pestering for sexual favours.

In summary, it is important to bear in mind that an employer could face claims of unlawful harassment at tribunal whenever:

- someone engages in sexist remarks, coarse or vulgar humour, racial jokes, racist or homophobic banter, jokes about religious views or practices, or jokes or remarks about people with disabilities in the workplace, and

- as a result, another employee finds the working environment offensive or otherwise unacceptable.

It is irrelevant whether or not the perpetrator of the remarks or banter intended to cause offence, as the question of whether behaviour amounts to harassment depends on the perception of the person on the receiving end.

Non-verbal harassment

Non-verbal harassment may include:

- the display of pin-up calendars on the wall, which some women may find demeaning or otherwise unacceptable

- sexually explicit or racist material displayed on computer screens, for example certain types of screensaver

- offensive gestures

- leering in an overtly sexual manner

- persistently staring at a disabled person

- the conspicuous display of a tattoo or the wearing of a badge that contains a slogan that is racist or offensive to people of a particular religion.

Clearly employers should have rules in place to ban such behaviour in the workplace.

The likely effects of harassment/bullying in the workplace

The effects of harassment or bullying in the workplace can be extremely serious, both for the employer and for the employee.

The practical effects of harassment and bullying at work

Harassment of any kind can have devastating effects on the person who is subjected to it, and may also create a working atmosphere of fear and oppression in which employees will not be able to perform at their best. An individual who is the victim of harassment may lose confidence, feel anxious and unhappy, and the stress caused by the harassment may even cause serious illness.

From the employer's perspective:

- Reduced motivation is likely to lead to poorer performance and productivity generally.

- Increased levels of absence are likely along with the associated costs of statutory and contractual sick pay.

- The organisation is likely to experience higher staff turnover.

Furthermore, an employee who is being bullied by a supervisor will inevitably fear the bully and may consequently be reluctant to raise work problems and be inhibited from putting forward constructive ideas for fear of being ridiculed or put down.

There may also be claims to employment tribunals (see next section) causing considerable inconvenience, diversion of resources, embarrassment if the case becomes public knowledge, general hassle and of course the likely expense, especially if the case succeeds.

Legal consequences

An employee who is exposed to harassment or bullying at work may choose to use the anti-discrimination legislation to make a straightforward claim for unlawful harassment or, if the behaviour that has caused offence is not linked to sex, sexual orientation, race, religion or disability, may choose to resign and claim constructive dismissal. Both of these are discussed below.

Claims to tribunals for unlawful harassment

Employers are liable in law for any act of discriminatory harassment carried out by one employee against another in the course of their employment (see below under 'Employers' liability for harassment under discrimination legislation'). Thus any workers who believe that they are being exposed to unlawful harassment in the workplace can bring a complaint against their employers to an employment tribunal under the relevant discrimination statute. There is no minimum length of service requirement for bringing a case of discrimination to a tribunal, and no age limit. If a claim succeeds, the employer will in most cases be ordered to pay the complainant compensation for financial loss (if any) and for injury to feelings.

Liability cannot be avoided by pleading ignorance of the fact that the harassment was taking place, or by asserting that there was no deliberate intention to offend the victim. In *Canniffe v East Riding of Yorkshire Council [2000] IRLR 555*, it was held that even where an employer has taken steps to prevent discrimination, for example by introducing an anti-harassment policy, it is appropriate to examine whether there were any further preventative steps that the employer could have taken that were reasonably practicable. If further steps could have been taken but were not, the employer will be held liable.

The possibility of a claim for constructive dismissal

An employee who is being seriously harassed or bullied at work may be able to succeed in a complaint of constructive dismissal based on the assertion that the way in which he or she was treated was intolerable to the extent that it amounted to a fundamental breach of contract and left no alternative but resignation.

Serious bullying or harassment, or a failure on the part of management to deal adequately with a genuine complaint of such behaviour, would in most cases be regarded by the courts as a breach of trust and confidence, a duty that exists within every contract of employment.

To succeed in a claim for constructive dismissal:

- There must have been a fundamental breach of contract.

- The employee must have resigned because of the breach of contract, and not for some other reason.

- The employee must have resigned promptly following the breach.

- The employee must have a minimum of one year's continuous service with the employer to be eligible to take such a claim to an employment tribunal.

- The employee must normally lodge the claim within three months of resigning.

In *Morrow v Safeway Stores plc EAT 275/00*, the EAT held that a breach of the implied term of trust and confidence would always amount to a fundamental or repudiatory breach of the employee's contract.

Employers' liability for harassment under discrimination legislation

Discrimination legislation very clearly places responsibility on employers for any discriminatory actions on the part of their workers. For example, the Sex Discrimination Act 1975 s.41(1) states:

> Anything done by a person in the course of his employment shall be treated for the purposes of this Act as done by his employer as well as by him, whether or not it was done with the employer's knowledge or approval.

Similar wording appears in all the other anti-discrimination statutes. This means in effect that, whenever an individual says or does something discriminatory 'in the course of employment', the employer may be held liable in law for any detrimental effect that such conduct has on any other worker. Ignorance of the fact that discrimination was taking place will not provide the employer with a defence, nor will it be a defence for the employer to argue that there was no intention to discriminate.

The phrase 'in the course of employment' has been interpreted widely by courts and tribunals, and employers may wish to note that it is likely to be interpreted to include behaviour that occurs at organised work-related events, whether social or otherwise. Such events could include, for example, the annual Christmas party or a residential training course held over a weekend. This will be irrespective of whether the event took place on work premises or at an external venue.

Individual employees' potential liability for harassment

Although the principle claim for discrimination or harassment occurring in the course of employment must be taken against the employer, it is also open to the complainant to name one or more individuals whom he or she believes were personally responsible for the harassment. It is not, however, possible to bring a case to an employment tribunal against a co-worker alone, as the principal case must be brought against the employer.

It is advisable therefore for employers to ensure that all their workers are made aware that they may be held personally accountable at an employment tribunal for any discriminatory conduct, and that they may have to pay compensation to their victim out of their own pockets if the case against them succeeds.

Harassment as a crime

In addition to the laws on discrimination that protect workers from harassment, the implementation of the Criminal Justice and Public Order Act 1994 in England and Wales made it a criminal offence for an individual to commit an act of deliberate harassment against another person. This Act does not apply in Scotland. To be covered by the Act, however, the harassment must be shown to have been intentional. This contrasts with the discrimination laws, under which a claim can be made out irrespective of whether there was a deliberate intention to harass the victim.

Specifically, it is an offence under the Criminal Justice and Public Order Act intentionally to commit an act that causes another person harassment, alarm or distress either:

- by using threatening, abusive or insulting language or behaviour, or disorderly behaviour, or

- by displaying any writing, sign or other visible representation that is threatening, abusive or insulting.

The Act covers all forms of harassment, irrespective of the motive behind it. It thus goes further than employment law to prohibit harassment on wider grounds, for example harassment motivated by personal dislike or a difference in political opinion. Thus an employee who is being intentionally harassed by a colleague at work may have recourse to justice by complaining directly to the police in addition to the potential right to bring a complaint against the employer to a tribunal alleging discrimination on one of the prohibited grounds.

Another criminal law governing harassment that applies throughout the United Kingdom is the Protection from Harassment Act 1997. This Act makes it a criminal offence to pursue (on two or more occasions) a course of conduct that amounts to harassment, or causes a person to fear that violence will be used against him or her. The principal objective of this Act was to provide protection to individuals who were the victims of stalking. There is no requirement under this Act for the behaviour in question to be intentional for it to constitute an offence.

Furthermore, the Anti-terrorism, Crime and Security Act 2001 created an offence of religiously aggravated harassment. The Act amended the Crime and Disorder Act to include a new category of 'religiously aggravated criminal offences'. Thus harassment or hostility at work on the grounds of a person's membership of a religious group could be a criminal offence as well as affording the victim the opportunity to bring a claim against the employer for unlawful harassment under the Employment Equality (Religion or Belief) Regulations 2003. A 'religious group' is widely defined in the Act as 'a group of persons defined by reference to religious belief or lack of religious belief'.

What bullying is and is not

Bullying may be described as behaviour that is:

- threatening or intimidating

- abusive or offensive

- cruel or vindictive

- humiliating or degrading.

Bullying will inevitably erode its victim's confidence and self-esteem and is often linked to a persistent abuse of power, position or knowledge. Frequently, there is a manager/subordinate relationship between the person doing the bullying and the victim.

Examples of bullying behaviour could include:

- aggressive, intimidating or threatening behaviour

- insulting people or putting them down, especially if done in front of others

- direct verbal aggression, especially when accompanied by swear words

- deliberately imposing grossly excessive or unachievable workloads or impossible deadlines on individuals in order to put them at a disadvantage

- deliberately impeding someone's progress at work, for example by intentionally withholding important information

- victimising people by giving them only unpleasant or exceedingly trivial or menial tasks to do

- ostracising or openly ignoring an employee

- sending rude, intimidating or offensive messages to someone by e-mail

- repeated unfair and destructive criticism.

Although there is no anti-bullying employment law in force in Britain at present, an employee who is the victim of bullying, whether on a single occasion or in a series of incidents, may be able to succeed in a claim for constructive dismissal. One example of such a case was *Ogilvie v Neyrfor-Weir Ltd (Aberdeen) EAT Unreported 15 May 2003* (see 'Key case 1' in the box below, and also above under 'The possibility of a claim for constructive dismissal').

Key case 1

Ogilvie v Neyrfor-Weir Ltd EAT Unreported 15 May 2003

The employee, who worked as business development manager in an oil-related company, was required to travel overseas by his contract. Five days before Easter, he was told by his line manager that he would have to travel to Saudi Arabia over the holiday period to make a presentation. Normally, this would have been no problem, even with the short notice, but on this occasion it meant Mr Ogilvie would miss an important family reunion. Mr Ogilvie subsequently approached his line manager to see if he might be excused from making the trip. The line manager responded to this request in a very aggressive manner, swore at Mr Ogilvie and refused to entertain his request.

The following morning, Mr Ogilvie decided to try to persuade his manager to change his mind. There was a heated exchange between the two of them with the door open, during which the manager threatened Mr Ogilvie that if he did not make the trip, he would face the sack. To add insult to injury, the manager swore at him again and called him very insulting names, described later by the

---

EAT as the 'grossest language'. Later the same day, Mr Ogilvie tendered his resignation and subsequently claimed that the manager's behaviour constituted a breach of trust and confidence entitling him to resign and claim unfair constructive dismissal.

The case succeeded. Overturning the employment tribunal's decision, the EAT held that bad language of the type used in this case was unacceptable behaviour and amounted to a breach of trust and confidence entitling the employee to resign and claim constructive dismissal.

In contrast with some of the examples provided above, bullying cannot be defined primarily in terms of the employee's subjective feelings. Actions such as a reasoned discussion about a person's work standards, performance or attendance, which might include the asking of questions about the reasons for unsatisfactory performance or absence from work, or the giving of constructive, factual criticism, would not constitute bullying, even though the employee on the receiving end might not feel comfortable about what is happening. Similarly, allocating additional work or new duties to a reluctant employee or requiring someone to take more responsibility or change his or her behaviour would not constitute bullying unless such discussions were (for example) accompanied by aggressive or threatening behaviour and/or foul language.

The difference between bullying and a 'strong' management style

It is natural that people find it difficult to be on the receiving end of criticism or disciplinary action, or to be instructed to do something that they do not want to do. These things are, however, part of every manager's and supervisor's responsibilities, and do not of themselves constitute bullying.

Some key differences between bullying and a strong management style when dealing with conduct or performance are that:

- A strong management style would involve:
    - tackling any problems about employee's conduct or performance promptly and directly
    - telling the person plainly and in factual terms (but not aggressively) what the problem is and why it is a problem
    - remaining calm and adopting a reasonable manner and approach
    - listening actively to what the employee has to say on the matter
    - working with the employee to ascertain what can be done to improve conduct or performance
    - demonstrating to the employee that the manager is on his/her side.

- Bullying, in contrast, might involve:

  - getting emotional (for example, showing anger)

  - throwing insults at the employee

  - not explaining the reasons why the employee's conduct or performance is unsatisfactory, or how it impacts on others

  - refusing to listen to any explanations put forward by the employee

  - shouting or swearing

  - focusing on alleged personality defects rather than on facts

  - blaming the employee for whatever has gone wrong, rather than adopting a team approach

  - making generalised accusations, such as: 'You're always late with your work'.

An example of a case where the manager adopted a dictatorial management style which amounted to bullying occurred in *Horkulak v Cantor Fitzgerald International High Court [2003] IRLR 756* (see 'Key case 2 in the box below).

Key case 2

Horkulak v Cantor Fitzgerald International High Court [2003] IRLR 756

Mr Horkulak was engaged on a fixed-term contract as a senior broker. He earned £200,000 per annum, with the potential to earn about the same again in bonuses.

Mr Horkulak's manager adopted a dictatorial management style in relation to problems with his performance. The evidence was that the manager 'regularly employed strong, foul language and swear words and expressions containing expletives' and that he frequently threatened Mr Horkulak by threatening to dismiss him, accompanying this by swearing and the use of insulting and abusive names. This behaviour was described later by the court as a 'vicious and premeditated campaign of bullying, harassment and intimidation'. Mr Horkulak put up with it for a number of months, but ultimately suffered extreme stress and anxiety and eventually resigned. He brought a claim for wrongful constructive dismissal in the High Court.

The judge in the High Court found from the evidence that foul language was indeed frequently used in the workplace. The company tried to justify the manager's behaviour by arguing that abusive expressions and swear words were part of the culture of the workplace, and indeed the industry, and should be viewed as acceptable in the context of a fast-moving, high-pressure environment and the high level of pay that was earned.

The judge held, however, that frequent use of bad language 'did not sanitise its effect so as to remove its power to offend', that it was unacceptable, and that threats of dismissal should not be used to intimidate or issued in intemperate language.

The conclusion was that Mr Horkulak's position had become intolerable and that the manager's conduct towards him amounted to a breach of trust and confidence. Even though the employee worked in a high-pressure job with high demands on him and a high salary, this did not remove the duty on the manager to treat him fairly in relation to performance problems, or to deny him support.

Mr Horkulak was awarded almost £1 million in damages, based on salary and bonuses for two years and three months, the period up to the date when his fixed-term contract would have expired.

How to tackle a long-standing poor performance issue without being accused of bullying

One of the hardest problems a manager may ever have to face is the job of tackling poor performance that has been allowed to continue for a lengthy period of time, perhaps because a previous line manager chose not to address the problem or was afraid to do so. It would hardly be surprising, in these circumstances, if an employee (at least initially) took the view that the manager was acting unreasonably by criticising conduct or performance that had been condoned for months or even years.

A suggested approach to handling this situation is summarised below.

- The manager should set up an informal meeting with the employee, the main aim of which will be to make him or her aware that there are certain specific aspects of conduct or performance that the manager has noticed, and that appear to be unsatisfactory. The specific areas of dissatisfaction should be clearly identified and spelled out, with specific examples given of incidences where the employee has done something inappropriate or failed to do something that he or she should have done.

- If the employee (as is likely) retorts that 'no one has ever complained before' (or words to that effect), the manager should simply agree with that statement.

- The manager should reassure the employee that what has occurred in the past is in the past, and that no blame is being placed at anyone's door for past events, given that the previous manager did not raise the particular issue(s) or give any indication that there was a problem.

- The manager should then proceed to explain that, although what happened in the past is not open to criticism, the standards required in the future will have to be firmly established.

- The employee should then be informed of the standards and/or targets that are expected of all staff: for example, standards of time-keeping, the need to meet deadlines, sales targets, attendance requirements, levels of accuracy, safety standards (according to what is relevant in the particular case).

- The employee should be informed that the manager intends, having established what the standards or targets are, to monitor his or her conduct and/or performance over a defined period of time, for example the next three months.

- Following this first informal meeting, the employee's conduct or performance should be monitored closely. If there is a continuing failure to meet the standards or targets that were established at the meeting, the manager should proceed to instigate formal disciplinary or capability procedures.

- The manager should follow the organisation's procedures exactly, treating the employee firmly, but fairly at all times.

If, despite the above measures, the employee accuses the manager of bullying, the following procedure should apply:

- The manager should advise the employee that the accusation he or she is making is very serious, and explain that any accusation of bullying needs to be backed up by facts, which in turn must be viewed objectively.

- The manager should ask the employee precisely what he or she considers has been said or done that constitutes bullying. (It may be that the employee is making wild and unfounded accusations, in which case he or she will not be able to answer this question.)

- If the employee does give some examples of the manager's behaviour that he or she views as bullying, the manager should listen, take what is being said on board and consider objectively whether the criticisms are valid, before proceeding further.

- If it transpires that the employee may have a genuine complaint that the manager's treatment constitutes bullying, then the matter should of course be properly dealt with and resolved, ideally by a different manager.

- If satisfied that the accusation is unfounded, the manager should make it clear to the employee that making baseless claims of bullying is inappropriate, unhelpful and negative, and that such behaviour will not help to resolve the current problems

- Ask the employee to view what has happened objectively, rather than subjectively.

- Demonstrate some understanding as to why the employee feels aggrieved, for example by saying that it is understandable that he or she finds the situation difficult.

- Reassure the employee that the manager has every intention of treating everyone fairly, but that it is nevertheless unacceptable for any staff to perform or behave in a way that falls short of the employer's expected standards.

- Point out that it is the responsibility of every manager to ensure that all staff achieve the required standards, and that anyone who was falling short of these standards would be treated in the same way as the manager is now treating the employee.

- Ask the employee what support might be helpful, for example whether any coaching, mentoring or training would be appropriate.

- Reassure the employee that the manager is on his or her side and genuinely wants to give any support needed to help in reaching the required standards.

The difference between constructive and destructive criticism

It is part of every manager's and supervisor's role to provide feedback to employees about their performance, attendance, timekeeping and general conduct and standards. Such feedback may, from time to time, need to include the giving of criticism. This is an important managerial role whenever there is a need (or an opportunity) for an employee's performance, attendance or conduct to change or improve.

There is, however, a big difference between constructive and destructive criticism. Constructive criticism will focus on:

- actions and behaviour, focusing on what the employee has done or not done

- facts, with specific examples of behaviour that has been inappropriate and an explanation of why it was inappropriate

- future improvement, for example requiring the employee to do something differently or make changes.

Destructive criticism on the other hand may involve:

- aggressive behaviour, such as yelling

- personal insults or put downs

- allocating blame rather than responsibility

- focusing on how awful the situation is, rather than on future improvement or rectification of the problem.

Taking steps to prevent harassment and bullying in the workplace

Taking positive steps to prevent harassment in the workplace is much better than leaving things to chance. Where proper preventative measures are introduced, they will place the employer in a relatively strong position to defend any claims of unlawful harassment. This is because all the anti-discrimination laws include the statement that employers facing a claim for unlawful discrimination will have a defence if they can show that they 'took such steps as were reasonably practicable to prevent' the discrimination in question. This means that if the employers can provide evidence to a tribunal that they did everything they reasonably could to prevent harassment in the workplace, they may be held not liable for any harassment that does occur despite the measures taken. The burden of proving this defence is a high one, however, and tribunals will not only scrutinise employers' policies and procedures, but will examine the extent to which they were actually put into practice.

In order to prevent harassment or at least reduce the chance that it will occur, and minimise the likelihood of being held liable, employers should:

- devise and implement an equal opportunities policy and an anti-harassment policy that makes it clear that any form of harassment in the workplace is unacceptable

- thoroughly brief all employees about the policies and any accompanying procedures

- make sure all employees within the organisation are clearly advised of the types of behaviour that could constitute harassment (see 'Different forms of harassment' above)

- put rules in place to ban items such as pin-up calendars on the wall or screensavers that might cause offence

- train all managers and supervisors in equal opportunities matters and in harassment awareness, ensuring that they are equipped to identify the types of behaviour that can constitute harassment and deal adequately with any complaint

- monitor the implementation of the policies to ensure that they are being put into practice consistently.

Although the adoption of appropriate policies and procedures represents a very important first step in the journey towards protecting the employer from liability for claims of harassment, merely publishing a policy will not be enough on its own to protect against liability. In the event of a claim to tribunal for harassment, the tribunal will also examine closely whether:

- the policies and procedures genuinely have full management commitment and support

- the policies and procedures have been communicated properly to all staff in ways that ensure clear understanding

- management and (where relevant) staff have received adequate training

- disciplinary procedures have been amended so as to define harassment as serious misconduct.

It is important to understand that adopting and practising preventative measures is the only way that an employer will be able to escape liability for any act of harassment perpetrated by one of the company's workers.

However, it is also very important for employers to take prompt and decisive steps to deal with any instance of harassment as soon as they become aware of it. Taking appropriate measures to deal promptly and effectively with an allegation of harassment will not remove the employer's liability for the harassment in an overall sense, but it will play an important part in convincing a tribunal that, because the harassment was promptly investigated and dealt with, the employer had taken such steps as were reasonably practicable and necessary.

Another step that an employer may take to help identify any problems linked to bullying or harassment would be to conduct exit interviews whenever a member of staff resigns, in order to help identify any possible instances of problem relationships caused by or aggravated by bullying.

Model policy statement on harassment

The model policy statement on harassment shown in the box below could be used as part of an organisation's equal opportunities policy.

Dealing with instances of harassment and bullying if they occur

Managers and supervisors should be constantly vigilant to the possibility of bullying or harassment in the workplace. Managers should never assume that, just because no one has complained, no incidents of harassment are occurring. Nor should they adopt the attitude that they do not need to take any action until and unless someone complains. Instead they should be prepared to challenge any conduct that they see or

Model policy statement on harassment

As part of our commitment to equal opportunities, the Company aims to develop and encourage a working environment and culture in which harassment and bullying are neither tolerated nor acceptable and in which employees feel confident in coming forward to report any incidence of harassment. The Company adopts a zero-tolerance approach towards bullying and harassment.

It is the responsibility of management to ensure that this policy is upheld at all times. It is the responsibility of all members of staff to treat their colleagues with respect and dignity, and to ensure that their behaviour does not cause offence or upset to others.

Disciplinary action up to and including summary dismissal will be taken against any employee who is found to have harassed or bullied another person during the course of their employment.

Any employee who feels uncomfortable or distressed by the conduct of another person at work may raise the issue informally in the first instance with [nominated person] or alternatively invoke the Company's grievance procedure. No employee will be penalised in any way for raising a genuine complaint about harassment, and all complaints will be taken seriously.

hear that could indicate conflict between individuals, could be misconstrued or could cause offence, however slight. Such incidents should be followed up and, if necessary, dealt with in a way that ensures the employees involved understand the types of actions that may cause offence and why it is important to desist from such behaviour. It is much better for management to tackle any behaviour that could cause offence than to turn a blind eye and assume that the matter is insignificant or that it will resolve itself.

How to handle a complaint of bullying or harassment

If a complaint of bullying or harassment is received (whether formal or informal), the manager should always take what is being reported seriously in the first instance even if, at first glance, the complaint appears to be trivial or unfounded. It may be the manager's opinion that something that was said or done was trivial, but that does not mean that the employee who was the target or recipient of the behaviour was not offended or distressed by it. The manager should instead take an objective approach and seek to investigate and resolve the complaint promptly and effectively with the aim of putting a stop to any behaviour that has caused offence, embarrassment, intimidation or discomfort (and preventing its recurrence).

Procedure for dealing with complaints of bullying/harassment

- Check whether the employee who is alleged to have bullied or harassed someone has previously received any warnings for similar behaviour (or for other types of misconduct), and if so whether any earlier warnings are still in date.

- Consider suspending the person suspected of bullying/harassment for a short period of time to allow an investigation to take place. Such suspension should be on full pay.

- Interview any witnesses who may have knowledge about the employee's alleged bullying behaviour or who may have witnessed any of the alleged incidents.

- Write to the employee accused of bullying or harassment to invite him or her to a formal interview to discuss the matter. The letter should give full details of the allegations that have been made, including any evidence provided by witnesses.

- Allow the employee the right to be accompanied at the interview by a colleague or trade union representative.

- At the interview, allow the employee a full and fair opportunity to answer the allegations and/or provide an explanation for the conduct complained of. At this stage it should be made clear that the purpose of the discussion is to establish facts, not to make an accusation.

- If the employee puts forward information refuting the complaint, adjourn if necessary to consider the matter and possibly investigate further.

- Once the facts are on the table, try to establish whether the employee accepts or denies the allegations.

- Try to remain objective and to take a balanced approach to the information gained as a result of the investigation and the interview. Ensure that any personal views about the employee are not allowed to influence the overall assessment of what is alleged to have happened.

- Once discussions are concluded, adjourn and make a balanced decision about whether the employee did in fact behave in a way that constituted harassment or bullying.

- Communicate the outcome to the employee in writing, and, if the outcome is dismissal, inform the employee of the right of appeal.

- Keep confidential records of the investigation, any meetings with witnesses and the interview with the employee accused of bullying/harassment, and ensure these are handled in accordance with the Data Protection Act 1998.

- If, following the conclusion of proceedings, the harasser and the person whom he or she harassed continue to work in close proximity, monitor the situation to ensure that their working relationship is now harmonious, that no further instances of harassment have taken place and that neither party is engaging in recriminatory behaviour against the other.

Providing support for the employee who has been harassed

Any employee who has been the victim of bullying or harassment at work will inevitably have suffered distress and anxiety as a result of someone else's behaviour or actions. In particular, if harassment has been going on for a period of time, the adverse effect on the employee may be substantial. It may also have taken a considerable amount of courage to come forward to complain to management.

It follows that it will be very important, once it has been established that the employee has indeed been the victim of harassment, for the employer to offer full support to that person. This will of course include reassurance that the problem will be fairly and thoroughly dealt with, and a firm commitment to put a stop to the harassment, but may also involve the need to provide moral support to help the employee come to terms with what has happened.

One way of providing moral and practical support is to give the employee the opportunity to talk to a trained counsellor. This may be done either by appointing a member of staff who has received professional training in counselling techniques, or alternatively by providing employees with access to an external confidential advice service through an independent counselling organisation.

Dealing fairly with the perpetrator of harassment

Harassment of any kind in the workplace is a serious issue, and one that should always be treated seriously by management. However, it is important when dealing with an employee who is alleged to have harassed or bullied a colleague that the manager refrains from making accusations, showing emotion or jumping to premature conclusions. Someone accused of harassment has as much right to be treated fairly as the person complaining of it. As with any form of alleged misconduct in the workplace, it is important that the manager responsible for handling it should act fairly and reasonably in investigating and resolving the problem.

Nevertheless, instances of harassment will in some cases provide solid grounds for the perpetrator to be dismissed, while in other cases a formal written warning may be appropriate. Any warning issued should make it clear that any further type of harassment or victimisation of the complainant (or any other employee) is likely to lead to dismissal. By contrast, in cases where the individual was genuinely unaware that his or her conduct was causing offence, an informal warning may suffice so long as the person clearly understands and accepts that the conduct that was causing offence or embarrassment must not recur.

What if the victim refuses to continue to work alongside the erstwhile harasser?

If the type of harassment or bullying was not sufficiently serious to warrant dismissal, and even if it has been dealt with in some other appropriate way, there may still be an ongoing problem if the person who was the victim of the harassment is unwilling to continue to work alongside the perpetrator. It may be that this situation can be resolved by open communication, an apology from the person who committed the harassment combined with an open resolve not to repeat the behaviour that caused offence.

If this is not the case, the employer may have to consider other options, in particular if there has been a breakdown in trust between the parties. Essentially, the employer may have to consider transferring one or other of the people involved to another job or even another department.

If consideration is being given to transferring the employee who was the victim of harassment, the employer would have to be sure that person genuinely wished to move to another job, otherwise the transfer could be perceived as a discriminatory detriment. If, on the other hand, management wish to consider transferring the harasser to another post (as would be more appropriate if it had been established that the allegations of harassment were well-founded), the matter would still have to be discussed and agreed with him or her. To impose a transfer unilaterally without agreement would be likely to be a breach of the employee's contract, irrespective of the motive behind the transfer.

What to do if the employee will not consent to action being taken

An employee may come forward to a manager or to an HR manager to report an incident of bullying or harassment in confidence, but ask the manager to keep matters 'confidential' and not discuss the complaint with anyone else. This situation, although understandable from the perspective of the employee, who may feel embarrassed at the thought of the matter being disclosed or may fear retribution, poses a problem for management. If the person who hears the complaint respects the employee's wishes, he or she will be prevented from taking any action to put a stop to the bullying.

In a case such as this, it is usually preferable for the manager to try to persuade the employee that it is best for the matter to be taken forward in some way, whether formally or informally. The manager should point out that if nothing is done, the bullying or harassment is likely to continue and the situation may get worse. The employee should be assured of support and protection against any possible victimisation for having complained.

In some cases, it may be appropriate for the manager to take action without the employee's agreement. Such cases will be rare, but may be appropriate if the allegations of bullying or harassment are of a very serious nature or if the manager has grounds to believe that, if nothing is done, the employee may suffer extreme distress to the extent of becoming ill. Such a decision will not be taken lightly, but may be in the best interests of the employee, as well as the organisation, which may otherwise subsequently face a legal claim.

Where the employee is reluctant to agree to action being taken, the manager should open up the discussion with and explore the following options:

- The employee could speak to the harasser directly, identifying the behaviour that is unacceptable, explaining that it is causing offence and requesting it to stop.

- The employee could write a confidential note to the harasser/bully to the same effect.

- The manager could offer to help the employee work out what to say, or what to put in the letter, or could offer to be present when the employee approaches the bully, either as a witness or as facilitator.

- If the organisation employs a welfare officer or someone trained in confrontation and/or counselling techniques, that person could be brought into the frame, put fully in the picture and asked to speak to the harasser informally to explain that certain aspects of his or her conduct are causing offence or upset to the particular employee and asking the person to change the bullying behaviour.

- The employee could raise a formal grievance, in which case the matter would be properly investigated by management, and the allegations put to the alleged harasser at a formal interview (see above 'Dealing fairly with the perpetrator of harassment').

Whatever employees in such situations decide, it will be important to reassure them that they will not be penalised in any way on account of having complained about bullying or harassment, and that, if the harasser is spoken to by management, that person will be very clearly prohibited from saying or doing anything to victimise the employee for having complained.

Often, speaking directly to the person whose behaviour is causing offence is a very effective way to deal with bullying or harassment, unless the behaviour is of a very serious nature or relationships have broken down completely. In some cases, however, the harasser may not have realised that the behaviour is causing offence, or there may have been some misunderstanding or misinterpretation of things that have been said or done. If the matter is dealt with directly and informally on a face-to-face basis, it may be that the person will offer an apology and agree to change his or her behaviour, thus resolving the problem.

If, however, the employee decides to raise a formal grievance, he or she will need to provide the manager with details of the name of the perpetrator, the nature of the bullying or harassment (giving specific examples if possible), dates and times when incidents occurred, where they occurred, the names of any witnesses, and any action that the employee has already taken to try to stop the harassment.

Any employee who raises a genuine grievance over bullying or harassment should be reassured that:

- The allegations raised will be treated in confidence insofar as is possible (although complete confidentiality cannot be promised).

- The main aim of formal action will be to stop the harassment and prevent its recurrence.

- He or she will be supported throughout the time it takes to investigate and deal with the complaint.

- He or she will not be penalised or victimised in any way for having raised the complaint.

POINTS TO NOTE

- Harassment on grounds of sex, trans-gender status, race, religion or belief, sexual orientation or disability is regarded in law as a form of unlawful discrimination, giving the victim the right to bring a case to an employment tribunal.

- A complaint of harassment can be brought to a tribunal on the grounds that an employee's working environment was intimidating, hostile, degrading, humiliating or offensive to them on account of a colleague's conduct.

- A key principle in the laws governing harassment is that it is for each individual to determine what behaviour is acceptable to them and what they regard as offensive.

- A complaint of unlawful harassment can be taken to tribunal as a result of either a single serious incident or a series of relatively minor incidents, which, when viewed collectively, can be classed as a campaign of conduct amounting to unlawful harassment or causing detriment to the victim.

- Employers who do nothing to tackle the issue of workplace bullying/harassment are likely to experience reduced employee motivation, leading to poor performance and productivity, increased levels of sickness absence and higher staff turnover.

- Certain types of harassment may amount to criminal offences, over and above any liabilities under employment legislation.

- Although there is no anti-bullying employment law in force in Britain at present, an employee who is the victim of bullying, whether a single incident or a series of incidents, may be able to succeed in a claim for constructive dismissal.

- If employers have done everything that they reasonably could to prevent harassment in the workplace, they may be held not liable for an incident of harassment that does nevertheless occur in the workplace.

- It is much better for management to tackle any behaviour that could cause offence than to turn a blind eye, assume that the matter is insignificant or that it will resolve itself.

- The transfer of an employee to a different job or department following a complaint of bullying or harassment would probably be in breach of contract, irrespective of the motive behind the transfer, unless the employee's agreement to the transfer was first obtained.

- Speaking directly to the person whose behaviour is causing offence is often a very effective way to deal with behaviour that is perceived as bullying or harassment.

ACTION POINTS

- Recognise that bullying or harassment at work is a very significant issue that management in every organisation should take very seriously.

- Recognise that people are different, and that behaviour that one person finds funny or harmless may be offensive or embarrassing to someone else.

- Be vigilant to the dangers of verbal harassment in the workplace, for example sexist remarks, coarse or vulgar humour, racial jokes, racist or homophobic banter, jokes about religious views or practices, jokes or remarks about people with disabilities, or e-mails containing any of these.

- Make all workers aware that they may be held personally accountable at an employment tribunal for any discriminatory conduct, and that they may have to pay compensation to their victim out of their own pockets if a case of harassment succeeds.

- Recognise the differences between bullying and a strong management style when dealing with unsatisfactory employee performance or conduct.

- When tackling the problem of an employee whose unsatisfactory performance has been condoned for a long time, reassure the employee that no blame is being placed at his or her door for past events, but that the standards required of the employee in the future now need to be firmly established.

- Reassure employees whose performance is below the required standard that the management wishes to treat them fairly, is on their side and genuinely wants to support them so that they reach the required standards in the future.

- Develop a sound awareness of the differences between constructive and destructive criticism, and strive to ensure that any criticism of employees' performance or conduct is always wholly constructive.

- Make sure all employees within the organisation are clearly advised of the types of behaviour that could constitute harassment or bullying.

- Train all managers and supervisors in equal opportunities matters and in harassment awareness, ensuring that they are equipped to identify behaviour that could constitute harassment and to deal adequately with any complaint.

- Implement an anti-harassment/bullying policy and monitor its implementation to ensure that it is being put into practice consistently.

- Be prepared to challenge any conduct that could indicate conflict between individuals, be misconstrued or cause offence, however slight.

- Always take a complaint of bullying or harassment seriously and investigate it thoroughly, even if at first glance the complaint appears to be trivial or unfounded.

- Allow any employees accused of bullying or harassment a full and fair opportunity to answer the allegations against them, and/or provide an explanation for their conduct, at a properly convened interview.

- Offer full support to any employee who has been the victim of bullying or harassment at work, including reassurance that the problem will be fairly and thoroughly dealt with, the key aim being to put a stop to the harassment and prevent its recurrence.

- Reassure an employee who has come forward to complain about bullying or harassment that he or she will not be penalised or victimised in any way on account of having complained.

CHAPTER 5

ALCOHOL AND DRUGS

Introduction

Dealing with someone who has an alcohol or drug-related problem requires considerable skill, empathy and patience. On the one hand, an employee who has this kind of problem may be guilty of misconduct such as persistent lateness, but on the other hand he or she may also be genuinely ill and in need of support.

Abuse of drugs or alcohol can lead to problems in the workplace such as:

- deterioration of work performance

- high levels of absence

- poor timekeeping

- workplace stress

- potential risks to the safety of the employee or his/her colleagues

- accidents at work

- damage to the organisation's reputation

- increased staff turnover.

A problem related to an employee's abuse of alcohol or illegal drugs should never be ignored, but instead should be tackled in a positive, supportive and fair manner.

Employers may wish to consider introducing a policy on drugs and alcohol, including a programme of positive action and (if justified) an alcohol/drug screening programme.

This chapter aims to address how management should deal with an employee who is believed or known to have a problem with alcohol or illegal drugs.

Managing an employee who has an alcohol or drug-related problem

Most line managers, and many HR professionals will find it difficult to tackle the problem of an employee who uses drugs or over-uses alcohol. The condition may manifest itself in the workplace in deteriorating job performance, regular lateness, frequent days off work, and/or erratic or moody behaviour. While these problems clearly create a predicament for line managers, it is important to exhibit some tolerance towards the employee where he or she is genuinely ill.

Various issues may arise. Among other problems, the employee may:

- appear to be under the influence of alcohol while at work, or come to work hung-over, which in turn would adversely affect performance and may endanger safety

- be a regular drug user, which may (or may not) affect performance, attendance or conduct

- become drunk (and possibly disruptive or even abusive) at a work-related social function

- be seen taking illegal drugs at a work-related function

- be accused of illegal drug taking outside work, in which case the employer would need to assess whether or not that was in any way relevant to the his or her job.

The first and most important question for the employer to establish is whether the employee is addicted to alcohol or drugs (in which case he or she should be regarded as 'sick' and dealt with under a 'capability procedure') or whether the alcohol or drug-related behaviour represents misconduct (i.e. the person is not an addict but has taken drugs or become drunk in circumstances that adversely affect his or her employment).

It is worth noting that neither alcohol dependency nor addiction to an illegal drug is classed as a disability under the Disability Discrimination Act 1995. There is one exception to this principle, which is a dependency on a drug that has been medically prescribed.

Whether to apply capability or conduct procedures

When a manager first becomes aware of signs or symptoms that indicate that someone's performance, conduct or attendance at work is affected by alcohol or drugs, steps should be taken to establish whether the problem is one of capability or conduct.

The term 'capability' in employment law terms covers ill health (among other things). Thus if an employee is an alcoholic or has become addicted to a particular drug, it would be necessary to treat that person according to the same principles as would be applied to any other staff suffering from serious illness that affected their work. Thus if someone's job performance is deteriorating, or if his or her attendance has become unreliable or erratic, and if there are indications that these factors might be linked to alcohol or drug use, then the matter should be treated as a capability issue in the first instance. The key principle is that if an employee is ill, the overall approach should be one of support rather than blame, and so disciplinary action would not be appropriate. It follows also that a dismissal for lack of capability in these circumstances would be unlikely to be fair until the employer had exhausted all other possibilities, such as the provision of support, counselling and time off to rehabilitate.

If, however, the matter is one of misconduct, it would be appropriate to deal with it under the organisation's normal disciplinary procedure; that is to say, the employer should put the alleged misconduct in writing, hold a meeting with the employee to discuss the matter, and allow the right of appeal against any disciplinary outcome. Such a course of action may be appropriate, for example, in the case of an isolated incident of unauthorised time off that was due to heavy drinking. Alternatively if a single very serious incident occurs, for example violence at work as a result of the person being under the influence of drink or drugs, then this would be regarded as gross misconduct justifying summary dismissal. For example, in *Evans v Bass North Ltd EAT 715/86*, an employment tribunal ruled that it was fair for the employer (who ran a restaurant) to dismiss a chef with 11 years service following an incident in which the chef was drinking in the kitchen and threatened the manager with a knife. This was despite the fact that the chef was a recognised alcoholic. Manifestations of an employee's alcohol problem that take the form of gross misconduct may be treated as such, depending on the circumstances of the particular case.

An employer should therefore adopt different approaches and procedures, depending on whether the matter being dealt with is one of capability or conduct. Equally, if the matter is one of misconduct, a distinction should be drawn between incidents of gross misconduct, which may (depending on the circumstances) justify summary dismissal, and less serious misconduct, which should be treated with sympathy if linked to the employee's addiction. If there is any doubt, the employer should normally give the employee the benefit of the doubt in the first instance and regard the matter as one of capability.

Why distinguishing between capability and conduct is important

The distinction between capability and conduct is important, not only to ensure fair and reasonable treatment of someone who has an addiction to alcohol or illegal drugs, but also in the event that an employee is eventually dismissed for an alcohol or drug-related reason. If a claim of unfair dismissal goes to a hearing, the onus will be on the employer to prove the reason for the employee's dismissal. If employers cite the 'wrong' reason, they will lose the case. For example if an employee who is an alcoholic has been dismissed ostensibly on the grounds of misconduct, but can provide medical evidence of an addiction to alcohol and can link the 'misconduct' to the addiction, the tribunal may find that the employer did not have a good reason for the dismissal, or alternatively that it acted unreasonably in dismissing the employee for this reason.

Tribunals have tended to distinguish between dismissals on grounds of an employee's use of hard drugs (which are generally viewed as capability dismissals since such drugs are addictive) and those related to soft drugs. Thus the reason for a dismissal on grounds of (for example) use of cannabis would usually be regarded as misconduct rather than capability; in other words, the use of soft drugs is often viewed as a wilful act of misconduct rather than as an illness.

Dealing with an employee who refuses to acknowledge that there is a problem

Where an employer has initially treated the matter as one of capability and offered support, but the employee refuses to acknowledge that he or she has a problem with alcohol or drugs, the employer may then regard any further instances of inappropriate behaviour on account of alcohol or drug use as misconduct.

It will, however, be very important in these circumstances for the employer to advise the employee clearly and specifically that any further instances of unsatisfactory job performance, behaviour or attendance will be dealt with as misconduct, and will result in disciplinary proceedings. This should also be confirmed in writing. The employee should also be advised unambiguously if there is any possibility that unsatisfactory conduct, performance or attendance could eventually lead to dismissal.

Dealing with an employee who accepts support but fails to improve

Although it is good practice for an employer to provide support to an employee with an alcohol or drug addiction, it should be made clear in writing at the outset of the rehabilitation programme that continued support and sympathetic treatment will depend on the employee following through any course of medical treatment that has been agreed.

Thus if someone has admitted to having a drink or drug problem and has accepted the organisation's offer of support and rehabilitation, but fails to stick with the rehabilitation programme, fails to improve or lapses back into old habits part-way through or at the conclusion of the programme, it may be fair for the employer to regard any further instance of unsatisfactory conduct or performance caused by alcohol or use of drugs as misconduct. Again, the employee should be clearly advised in writing of the employer's change of approach and the reasons for it.

Offering support where the employee is thought to have an addiction

Where an employee's drinking or drug taking has turned into an addiction or is associated with a medical condition (such as depression), the matter should be regarded by the employer as a capability issue. The essential ingredient in the management of lack of capability is to afford the employee as much support as is reasonable in the circumstances. An appropriate course of action for the employer would therefore involve the following stages.

- Talk to the employee confidentially to try to establish whether he or she accepts that there is a problem, and that it is linked with alcohol or drugs. The person conducting the meeting should not be afraid to ask directly (but sympathetically) whether the employee has a problem with alcohol or drug use. Acknowledgement of the link with alcohol or drugs is an essential prerequisite to the success of any rehabilitation programme.

- Give support and reassurance that, provided the employee agrees there is a problem and is willing to cooperate to try to resolve it, the organisation will offer support and the opportunity of rehabilitation.

- Seek expert medical advice. Ideally this should be done by arranging for the employee to be interviewed and examined by an occupational doctor, who will be in a strong position to understand the likely affects of an alcohol or drug-related problem on the person's work. Alternatively, the employer could ask for consent to approach the employee's GP for a medical report in order to establish the nature of the problem, its effects, and the likelihood of a recovery. Chapter 8 discusses more fully the topic of obtaining medical advice.

- Taking into account medical advice, agree a programme of rehabilitation with the employee, together with timescales. The programme may involve the offer of time off work to undergo an agreed course of medical treatment and/or counselling (see 'Offering time off work and/or counselling' below).

- Consider the possibility of offering the employee reduced hours or lighter work (or, for example, work that is less stressful), at least on a temporary basis. If this is an option, ensure it is discussed and agreed directly with the employee. It is important to bear in mind that any change of hours or job duties implemented without clear consent would be a breach of contract.

- Agree time limits for improvement and for appraising the situation, and obtain the employee's agreement to the time limits.

- Agree not to institute (or continue) disciplinary action against the employee so long as he or she is willing to cooperate in working towards rehabilitation.

Offering time off work and/or counselling

If an employee has admitted to a problem linked to alcohol or drugs, a course of action leading potentially to rehabilitation should be discussed with him or her with a view to agreeing the way ahead.

Taking into account medical advice, the employer may wish to offer the employee time off work in order to undergo an agreed course of medical treatment and/or counselling. This may involve a period of paid sickness absence, or alternatively an agreement for time off each week (for example a day or half a day) to attend appointments and undergo treatment.

It will be important to agree with the employee:

- how much time off work is to be permitted

- over what period of time it will be permitted

- what type of rehabilitation programme is to be undertaken

- how the employer is to be kept informed of the employee's progress.

Dismissal

Dismissal of an employee on grounds of genuine ill health can be fair under the Employment Rights Act 1996, s.98(2–3), provided it is reasonable for the employer to treat the matter as one justifying dismissal. Whether dismissal is reasonable will depend on many factors, which are discussed in the section on 'The last resort: dismissal' in Chapter 7.

There is no specified period of time in law after which it is fair to dismiss an employee who is ill on account of an alcohol or drug addiction. The basic question that determines fairness (or unfairness) in a dismissal for ill health is whether in all the circumstances employers can reasonably be expected, in light of their business requirements, to wait any longer for an employee to recover and resume effective working. Employers are not expected to put up with absenteeism and drink/drug-related problems indefinitely. Factors that would be taken into account by an employment tribunal when assessing a claim for unfair dismissal of this type include:

- the size and resources of the employer

- the degree of disruption the employee's problem is causing the organisation

- the level of seniority or degree of specialisation of the employee's job

- any possible negative impact on the customers of the business, or on the employer's reputation

- the feasibility of employing a temporary replacement while the employee is granted time off for rehabilitation

- the level of support afforded to the employee prior to the decision to dismiss

- the level of cooperation demonstrated by the employee in relation to the employer's offer of support and rehabilitation.

Addressing the problem of an employee whose over-indulgence in alcohol affects attendance, performance or conduct

Someone who has an alcohol addiction or who drinks heavily, whether regularly or on an occasional basis, may present a variety of problems for an employer. Such problems could include:

- drinking alcohol while at work

- being under the influence of alcohol at work

- being hung-over at work.

Alcohol at work

All employers should have, as part of their disciplinary code or rules, a statement that no one is permitted to have alcohol in his or her personal possession at the workplace. It should also be made clear in the disciplinary code that any breach of this rule will be regarded as misconduct leading to disciplinary action.

Employers should note that under the Health and Safety at Work Act 1974, an employer can be prosecuted for knowingly allowing an intoxicated employee to continue working.

The actual consumption of alcohol while on duty should also be specified as a disciplinary offence. In most, if not all, workplaces, it will be appropriate to list drinking alcohol at work as gross misconduct. The rules should be clearly communicated to all staff, who must be told unambiguously and in writing that any alcohol consumption at work will be regarded as gross misconduct leading to summary dismissal following even a first offence.

Different employers may take different approaches to the question of whether alcohol should be condoned or prohibited during an employee's lunch break. Again the rules should be made absolutely clear so that there can be no room for doubt or misinterpretation on the part of employees. Where, for example, a job involves entertaining clients, it would normally not be appropriate to ban lunchtime drinks, but the policy could still state that over-indulgence in alcohol to the extent that the employee becomes intoxicated is a disciplinary offence.

If a blanket ban on alcohol at work is imposed, the employer should adopt an attitude consistent with the policy and should not, for example, provide alcoholic drink at business lunches or meetings. Equally, in the interests of consistency, a complete ban on alcohol must be applied to all staff, including senior managers.

Even where clear rules are in place banning alcohol, if a drink-related incident occurs in the workplace, it will still be advisable to consider, through investigation and discussion, whether the employee may have an inherent health problem involving alcohol (see above 'Whether to apply capability or conduct procedures'). Even though the organisation's code of conduct may state clearly that use of alcohol at work will be grounds for summary dismissal, that does not mean that the employer should automatically dismiss an employee who breaches the rule. Fairness demands that each case must be considered on its individual merits, and where the employee is an alcoholic or drug addict, this will be a mitigating factor that the employer needs to take into account.

An employee who appears to be under the influence of alcohol at work

Although it is appropriate to treat anyone who is known to be an alcoholic with patience and sympathy, this does not mean that the employer must tolerate the inappropriate conduct of an employee who comes to work under the influence of alcohol. The employer should in the first instance consider whether the behaviour is due to alcoholism or associated illness (such as depression), rather than being wilful misconduct. If this is the case, dismissal would be unlikely to be fair unless the employer had first offered the employee support and the opportunity for rehabilitation (see above, 'Offering support where the employee is thought to have an addiction').

When drunkenness at work may constitute grounds for summary dismissal

Where a first offence of drunkenness at work is very serious, the employer may be entitled to regard it as gross misconduct justifying summary dismissal. Examples could include gross negligence in the carrying out of duties, fighting, abusive behaviour towards colleagues or customers, or a breach of safety rules as a result of being drunk.

Summary dismissal may thus be appropriate even in circumstances where the employee is addicted to alcohol, especially where the nature of the job or the working environment is such that the consumption of alcohol or its effects could give rise to a serious safety risk. Under the Health and Safety at Work Act 1974, employers are obliged to take reasonable steps to ensure that their employees are not acting under the influence of alcohol or drugs if this is likely to place the health and safety of others at risk.

Whether it is reasonable for the employer to regard drunkenness at work as gross misconduct justifying summary dismissal will depend on all the circumstances of the individual case, including:

- whether the employee has an addiction to alcohol and if so the extent to which this should be regarded as a mitigating factor

- the employee's position and level of responsibility in the organisation

- whether the job involves contact with clients or customers

- the specific duties of the job, particularly if it is safety-sensitive

- whether there are any special mitigating factors put forward by the employee (for example a recent bereavement)

- medical evidence

- the context.

In assessing the seriousness of an employee's misconduct associated with drinking alcohol, the employer should take the context into account. For example, while it would potentially be reasonable to dismiss someone for being under the influence of alcohol where his or her condition posed a safety risk to colleagues, it would be unreasonable (and almost certainly unfair) to dismiss a desk-based worker for being mildly tipsy at work after a department lunch on Christmas Eve.

Distinguishing between misconduct and gross misconduct

Employers should distinguish between routine misconduct caused by alcoholism, such as poor attendance, lateness or poor work standards – which should be treated sympathetically – and serious misconduct caused by alcoholism, such as lack of attention to safety standards or abusive behaviour at work, which may (depending on the circumstances) justify summary dismissal. Even so, employers should always view an employee's alcoholism as a mitigating factor, otherwise a dismissal may be unfair.

Following fair procedures

Irrespective of the nature or seriousness of the employee's conduct, the employer should (before deciding on disciplinary action or dismissal):

- investigate the matter fully

- inform the employee in writing of the allegations, inviting him or her to attend a disciplinary hearing

- offer the right to be accompanied at the hearing by a colleague or trade union official of the employee's choice

- during the hearing, put any evidence to the employee in full, offering a full and fair opportunity to answer the case and put forward any explanations

- communicate the outcome of the disciplinary action in writing

- allow a right of appeal against any decision to dismiss or impose a disciplinary sanction.

Uncertainty as to whether an employee is under the influence of alcohol

One obvious problem in dealing fairly with employees who appear to be under the influence of alcohol at work is the difficulty of knowing whether their condition or behaviour is in fact related to alcohol. The employer should refrain from making uninformed assumptions about an employee who may, for example be taking prescribed medication that has side effects (such as drowsiness) rather than being drunk on duty. The manager should approach the matter in an open and non-judgemental way and carry out prompt investigations into the employee's conduct.

Appropriate investigations may include:

- speaking to the employee confidentially, pointing out the behaviour or symptoms that have been noticed and asking for an explanation

- if appropriate (and depending on whether the employer operates a drug/alcohol screening policy), bringing in a qualified person to examine the employee or carry out a test (for example, a breath test) to determine the presence or absence of alcohol

- taking statements from any witnesses with respect to the employee's conduct

- if there are no witnesses, and there is no opportunity to have a qualified person examine the employee, seeking the support of a colleague (for example a senior manager or HR professional) to observe his or her condition and form an objective opinion about it.

Suspension from work

In most cases, if there are grounds to believe that an employee is under the influence of alcohol at work, it will be appropriate to suspend that person from work immediately. Suspension should be on full pay unless the employee's contract expressly permits suspension without pay in these precise circumstances. Even if this is the case within a particular workplace, suspension without pay would be an extremely risky strategy because the employee would be entitled to view such treatment as an indication that the employer had already assumed a guilty verdict without first investigating the matter. This in turn could be viewed as a breach of trust and confidence in the employment relationship, entitling the employee to resign and claim constructive dismissal (subject to having a minimum of one year's continuous service with the employer).

An employee who is hung-over at work

Depending on the nature of the employer's business and the type of duties that the employee is engaged to do, coming to work with a hangover could be seriously detrimental to a person's performance or even to workplace safety. Where the job involves, for example, the operation of machinery, responsibility for the care of other people, or driving duties, the employer may wish to impose restrictions on the consumption of alcohol within off-duty periods so as to ensure employees are not hung-over when they come to work.

Such a rule would represent a breach of the employee's right to privacy under Article 8 of the Human Rights Act 1998, but could nevertheless be potentially justified if there were safety reasons for the rule (see below under 'Human rights implications on banning alcohol or drug taking in private time').

Drinking while on call

If employees are required as part of their contracts to be on call at set times, the employer should consider whether to impose rules as to the consumption of alcohol during on-call periods. It may be advisable to ban alcohol during such periods, particularly if a call out would involve a requirement for the employee to drive in order to carry out the necessary duties.

Drunkenness outside work

It will not normally be appropriate for an employer to impose rules on employees' use of alcohol in their own private time, except in the sorts of circumstances listed below in 'Rules on drinking alcohol'.

Nevertheless, if an employee becomes drunk in his or her own time and as a result behaves in a way that would be likely to bring the employer into ill repute, or cause embarrassment with a customer, the employer may be justified in taking disciplinary action.

For example in *Raylor v McArdle EAT 573/84*, the EAT ruled that a worker's dismissal following an incident where he was observed to have been 'legless' on a building site was fair, even though he was off-duty at the time. The dismissal was fair because the employer was able to demonstrate that his condition would undermine the confidence of the site agents.

Rules on drinking alcohol

All employers should devise and implement clear rules on the consumption of alcohol during working time and specifying:

- any specific time period (e.g. eight hours) prior to the commencement of work where, for example, the job involves driving or is otherwise safety-sensitive

- whether drinking alcohol during lunch breaks is permitted or forbidden

- whether employees are banned from drinking alcohol while on call

- any rules about drinking alcohol at work-related events such as social functions, for example a rule stating that employees must not become drunk (see below, 'Dealing with drunkenness or drug taking at work-related functions')

- a rule that employees must not, in their own time, behave in any way that would be likely to bring the organisation's name into ill repute, for example through excessive drinking in a public place

- the penalties for breach of these rules.

Tackling employees' drug taking that affects attendance, performance or conduct

The use of illegal drugs such as heroin, cocaine or cannabis, or the misuse of legally prescribed drugs, may or may not affect an employee's attendance, job performance or conduct at work. If it can be shown that drug taking does affect attendance, performance or conduct, the employer would be entitled to regard the matter as one of capability or misconduct, depending on the circumstances (see above 'Whether to apply capability or conduct procedures').

Drug taking at work

Since it is a criminal offence for an individual to use or distribute controlled drugs, the employer would be justified in regarding any instance of illegal drugs at the workplace as gross misconduct. Nevertheless it is advisable for employers to have a clear policy statement that the possession, use or supply of illegal drugs at work is strictly forbidden. This would be in order to avoid the possibility, however slight, of an employee succeeding in a case of unfair dismissal on the grounds that he or she was unaware that such conduct would lead to dismissal.

Employers should also be aware that they will be committing a criminal offence under the Misuse of Drugs Act 1971 if they know that illegal drugs are being kept, supplied or used on their premises.

Employees' outside-work drug taking and whether it is any concern of the employer

From an employment law perspective, drug taking outside work is more likely to be regarded as misconduct than alcohol consumption. This is primarily because the use of drugs is a criminal offence, while drinking alcohol (even in excess) is not against the law. Nevertheless, it cannot be assumed that an employee who consumes an illegal substance outside work is guilty of misconduct, or that the employer has the right to interfere with what employees choose to do in their private lives.

It follows that recreational use of drugs outside work may or may not constitute grounds for disciplinary action, depending on the employer's policies and rules (if any) and on the impact, or likely impact, an employee's drug taking has or might have on that person's employment. On the one hand, the employer has a duty to ensure a safe workplace and a right to expect staff to perform their jobs to a high standard, while on the other hand there is no right for the employer to interfere unjustifiably in their private lives.

Whether an employee's outside-work drug taking impacts on performance, conduct or attendance

The key issue in determining whether it is appropriate for an employer to take action on grounds of an employee's recreational use of drugs is whether there is, or is likely to be, an adverse effect on that person's performance, conduct or attendance as a consequence of the drugs. This of course is hard to establish in individual cases, and managers should avoid making blanket assumptions, applying moral standards or judging others in light of their own personal views. Occasions when disciplinary action would be appropriate could include circumstances where:

- Impaired performance could lead to a safety risk (however slight).

- The employee's job requires intense concentration (which could again lead to a safety risk if, for example, his or her level of alertness is likely to be impaired).

- The job involves working with machinery.

- The employee's job entails responsibility for the care of others (for example someone employed to drive, or to supervise young people or vulnerable adults).

It is advisable for employers whose employees perform jobs that fit into any of the above categories to devise and implement clear rules that ban them from consuming illegal drugs in their own time, and to make it clear that an employee who is found to have breached the rules will be liable to summary dismissal for gross misconduct.

Before embarking on disciplinary action on account of the effects of drug taking on an employee's conduct, attendance or performance, employers should bear in mind that the use of illegal drugs may be linked to depression, which is of course an illness (and may also be a disability under the Disability Discrimination Act 1995). It will therefore be advisable to obtain medical advice about the employee before instituting disciplinary action, and especially before taking a decision to dismiss.

Human rights implications on banning alcohol or drug taking in private time

A ban on employees taking drugs in their own private time would constitute an invasion of individuals' rights to a private life under Article 8 of the Human Rights Act 1998.

The right to privacy may, however, be legitimately restricted in certain defined circumstances, namely if the restriction is imposed for the purpose of:

• national security

• public safety

• the prevention of disorder or crime

• the protection of health or morals

• the protection of the 'rights and freedoms' of others.

'Others' in this context includes the employer and co-workers. It could be argued, for example, that an employer has a 'right' to expect employees to fulfil their duties competently and effectively.

The fundamental question under human rights principles is whether interference with an employee's right to a private life is designed to achieve a legitimate business aim, and is proportionate to the achievement of that aim. 'Proportionate' has been defined in human rights term as meaning 'appropriate and necessary'.

It would be unquestionably accepted, for example, that safety in the workplace was a legitimate aim. Whether a ban on employees taking drugs outside work in their own time was proportionate to the achievement of that aim would depend on the nature of the employee's job and whether there was a realistic likelihood that leisure-time drug taking could compromise workplace safety. For example, it would in all likelihood be proportionate to impose a rule banning drug taking outside work for staff who were employed to drive vehicles, while the imposition of a similar ban on the same employer's office-based personnel would not be appropriate because there would, arguably, be no realistic safety implications.

The same principles would apply to an employer who imposed a ban on employees drinking alcohol during on-call periods, or within set time periods prior to coming on duty.

In *Whitefield v General Medical Council [2003] IRLR 39*, a doctor who had depression and abused alcohol, was ordered by the General Medical Council to stop drinking or else lose his registration. The doctor did not stop drinking, however, and was subsequently suspended for 10 months during which time he had to stop drinking and attend a support group, and could only work for 30 hours a week under supervision. He claimed this course of action amounted to a breach of his rights under Article 8 of the Human Rights Act 1998. The House of Lords decided ultimately that although there had been a breach of the employee's right to a private life under Article 8, it was overridden by public safety concerns and hence justified.

Another important case, this time dealing with an employee's out-of-work drug taking was *O'Flynn v Airlinks the Airport Coach Co Ltd EAT 0269/01* (see 'Key case 1' in the box below).

Key case 1

O'Flynn v Airlinks the Airport Coach Co Ltd EAT 0269/01

Ms O'Flynn was employed as a customer-care assistant, but her job occasionally involved assisting drivers to manoeuvre coaches and serving hot drinks on moving coaches. The employer had introduced an alcohol and drugs policy, together with random screening. The policy ruled that employees were prohibited from having drugs or alcohol in their system while at work, and that a positive drugs test would lead to disciplinary action and possibly dismissal. The policy, and the consequences of a positive test result, had been well communicated to all staff.

Some five months after the introduction of the policy, Ms O'Flynn was selected for a random drugs test. She told the nurse who was carrying out the test that she had taken a number of substances over the previous weekend, including cocaine and cannabis. Her test proved positive for cannabis, but negative for cocaine. The employee was subsequently dismissed following a disciplinary interview. She claimed unfair dismissal.

The employment tribunal held the dismissal to be fair, and the EAT upheld this decision. Although the case occurred prior to the implementation of the Human Rights Act 1998, the EAT chose to consider the effect that Article 8

---

might have had on the outcome. They held that the employer's drugs screening policy infringed the employee's right to a private life to the extent that it meant that certain drugs could not be taken in her own time without jeopardising her employment, and because it required her to provide a urine sample if she was randomly selected for screening. Nevertheless, the EAT took the view that the policy and the testing were appropriate and necessary for reasons of public safety, and that Ms O'Flynn's dismissal following the positive test result and her admission that she had taken drugs was not disproportionate in light of the safety issues at stake. The ruling took into account the fact that the employee's job duties were safety-sensitive.

Whether dismissal for outside-work drug taking can be fair

In most cases, possession or use of drugs (especially soft drugs) outside work would not present a valid reason for the employer to take disciplinary action against the employee concerned. This would be the case unless the employer had a clear policy and rules in place to the effect that out-of-work drug taking would be regarded as a disciplinary offence leading potentially to dismissal.

If the employer learns that an employee has been convicted of a drugs offence outside work, the situation may be somewhat different. Criminal offences committed outside work may give rise to fair dismissal in circumstances where any one of the following criteria exists:

- where the employee's conduct outside work makes that person unsuitable, or unsafe, to perform the job he or she are employed to do (for example if the employee's job involves the supervision of vulnerable young people)

- where the offence undermines the employer's trust and confidence in the employee (for example where the employee is in a senior position)

- where there could be an adverse impact on the employer's reputation (for example where an employee accused of drugs use comes into regular contact with important customers)

- where the employee's drugs offence could have a seriously detrimental effect on relationships with colleagues.

An employee who is guilty of a drug offence outside work cannot be automatically (fairly) dismissed solely because of being convicted or remanded in custody. If a dismissal is to be fair, there must be a link between the person's drug taking and his or her employment, such as one of the factors listed above. An instance of drug supplying, as opposed to drug using, would give the employer a stronger case to argue loss of trust and confidence in the employee, adverse impact on the employer's reputation, or detrimental effect on relationships with colleagues, thus potentially giving the employer grounds for dismissal.

The criteria listed above would also be relevant in the event of recreational drug taking that a manager discovers by chance. Thus, dismissal would be appropriate only where the incident or offence could be described as having a connection with the individual's employment.

As ever, the fairness of a dismissal will depend on all the circumstances of the individual case, and in particular the manner in which the employer has handled the issue. This will be more straightforward if the employer has a clear policy in place covering the question of drug taking outside work, including provision for dismissal in certain defined circumstances, usually where drug use could possibly impair the employee's performance or create a risk to safety.

Dealing with drunkenness or drug taking at work-related functions

As stated earlier (in 'Drug taking at work' above), since it is a criminal offence for an individual to use or distribute controlled drugs, it is advisable for employers to have a clear policy statement that the possession, use or supply of illegal drugs at work is strictly forbidden.

It is advisable also to extend this policy to work-related functions, which would include (for example) residential training courses, social functions held for the purpose of entertaining clients or customers, business lunches or annual Christmas parties. The policy should make it absolutely clear that any instance of an employee being found in possession of an illegal substance at any work-related function (whether on the employer's premises or at a private venue) will be regarded as gross misconduct and render the employee liable to summary dismissal. The policy should also state that over-indulgence in alcohol at a work-related function (for example an annual Christmas party) will not be tolerated and will similarly be regarded as gross misconduct.

With a clear policy in place, staff will understand clearly what behaviour is and is not acceptable at work-related events. If, subsequently, an employee does take drugs or becomes drunk and abusive at a work function, the employer would be able legitimately to take disciplinary action. The level of such action will of course depend on the person's behaviour and the circumstances in which it occurred. In particular, if misconduct takes place in front of clients or colleagues, or if an employee becomes aggressive or abusive when under the influence of alcohol, dismissal could be justified.

The fairness of a dismissal in these circumstances will of course depend on:

- the organisation's rules on the matter and whether they have been clearly communicated to staff

- the nature and seriousness of the employee's conduct at the function or event

- to what extent the employee's conduct at the function or event is likely to have a detrimental impact on his or her employment

- if the conduct was drink related, whether the employer provided a free bar or copious quantities of wine with dinner

- whether the employer has followed a fair and reasonable procedure prior to taking the decision to dismiss.

Key case 2

Focus DIY Ltd v Nicholson [1994] EAT 225/94

Ms Nicholson, who was a manager, openly smoked cannabis at a party held for staff and their guests at a local hotel. The party had been partly paid for by the company. Following a subsequent complaint about Ms Nicholson, she was interviewed and admitted that she had smoked cannabis. She was subsequently dismissed because the employer took the view that her conduct in smoking an illegal substance in front of junior colleagues had undermined her authority as a manager.

The EAT ruled that the dismissal was fair because the employer had genuinely lost trust and confidence in the employee's ability to manage staff as a result of her conduct.

Dismissal for drug taking at work functions is more likely to be deemed fair than dismissal for drinking, simply because the former is against the law.

Model policy on alcohol and drugs

Employers may wish to adopt the policy on alcohol and drug abuse shown in the box below.

Drug/alcohol screening policies

Drug and alcohol screening is not as common in the United Kingdom as it is in the United States; nevertheless, a number of UK companies have introduced screening in recent years.

Model policy on alcohol and drugs

It is the policy of the Company to offer support to any employee who suffers from a problem associated with use of alcohol or drugs. Support will include providing employees with information and encouragement to obtain specialist help. This policy applies to all staff.

The objectives of this policy are:

- to promote and maintain safety in the workplace

- to provide a framework for the prevention and management of alcohol and drug-related problems

- to provide an opportunity for any member of staff who has an alcohol or drug-related problem to seek and be provided with support.

Alcohol or drugs use can result in a number of problems both for the individual who is the user, and for the Company. For example, there may be:

- potential damage to the individual's health

- deterioration of work performance

- high levels of absence

- poor timekeeping

- workplace stress

- potential risks to the safety of the employee or his/her colleagues

- accidents at work

- damage to the organisation's reputation.

Any employee who believes or suspects that he or she may have an alcohol or drug-related problem is encouraged to speak confidentially to the company doctor/HR manager about the problem. Such information will be treated as confidential and the employer will not, in any circumstances, inform the police where an individual has disclosed information about use of illegal drugs. The employee will subsequently be afforded help and support in obtaining the appropriate medical treatment and counselling with a view to rehabilitation. Where necessary, paid time off work will be granted to undergo treatment.

Any line manager who has grounds to believe or suspect that an employee may have an alcohol or drug-related problem should take appropriate action to discuss the matter confidentially with the employee. Managers may draw conclusions about an employee's alcohol or drug problem as a result of observations of deteriorating work performance, unreliable attendance for no apparent reason, erratic time-keeping and/or behavioural problems. Such observations provide a manager with legitimate grounds to enter into discussions with the employee with a view to identifying the cause of the problem. Line managers may obtain advice on how to handle such a discussion from the HR manager, who will also sit in on the meeting with the employee if it is thought appropriate.

All employees of the Company have a duty to report any conduct or behaviour on the part of a colleague that they think may indicate alcohol or drugs abuse. An employee who makes such an observation should report the matter to his or her own line manager who will arrange to interview the individual concerned without revealing the identity of the person who provided the information.

The Company's policy of support includes:

- referral to an occupational doctor in the first instance

- referral to appropriate treatment agencies with the individual's consent and with the knowledge and agreement of the individual's GP

- appropriate time off work for such treatment

- payment of normal salary under the rules of the Company's sickness absence policy

- recognition of any periods of treatment as periods of sickness absence under the Company's sickness absence procedure

- possible modification to the employee's hours of work or job duties (if appropriate) during any period of treatment (with the employee's consent).

Provided the employee is willing to accept the Company's support to overcome a problem associated with use of alcohol or drugs, the Company will refrain from initiating, or will suspend, disciplinary proceedings. However, in the following circumstances, the individual will be liable to disciplinary action, up to and including dismissal:

- where the employee refuses to accept there is an alcohol or drug-related problem, but factors such as unsatisfactory job performance, poor attendance or unacceptable behaviour on the part of the employee indicate that such a problem may exist

- where the individual accepts that there is an alcohol or drug-related problem but refuses to accept the Company's offer of support

- where the individual embarks on a programme of medical treatment and rehabilitation, but fails to complete it

- where an individual has undertaken a course of treatment but subsequently relapses back into alcohol or drugs abuse. In this latter situation the Company may, at its discretion, provide further support and treatment.

Whether it is appropriate to implement screening

The key criterion when considering whether it is appropriate to implement alcohol/drug screening is whether an employee's use of alcohol or drugs would be likely to create a safety risk. The Health and Safety at Work Act 1974 places a general duty on every employer to 'ensure, so far as is reasonably practicable, the health, safety and welfare at work of all his employees'. This would include ensuring that staff are not acting under the influence of drugs (or alcohol) if this would be likely to risk the health and safety of themselves or others at work.

From an employment law standpoint, the purpose of an alcohol/drug screening programme should be to assess the competence of an employee to perform a specific job, not to control off-duty behaviour where the employee's work is not likely to be affected.

A further positive reason for introducing an alcohol/drug screening programme would be to provide a starting point for supporting any employee who had a drug/alcohol problem.

Organisations whose employees perform work in a hazardous environment (e.g. on offshore oil installations), work with machinery, or work in jobs where they are responsible for the care of others (e.g. drivers) would have solid grounds for introducing a compulsory alcohol/drug screening programme. While it would be inappropriate for any employer to intrude unnecessarily into the employees' private lives or personal conduct outside work, where such conduct could have an adverse impact on safety or job performance, then employers arguably need to take responsibility and appropriate action.

A company's screening programme for drugs and alcohol may involve:

- with cause testing, whereby a test is carried out only if there is an accident, incident or genuine suspicion that an employee is under the influence of alcohol or drugs at work

- voluntary random testing, subject to the employee's consent at the time

- compulsory random testing, where the policy is contractual and a refusal to agree to a test will constitute grounds for disciplinary action up to summary dismissal.

Human rights implications of screening policies

Whatever type of policy is introduced, the consent of the person concerned will be required before a test can be carried out (although a refusal without good reason may be grounds for disciplinary action, depending on the wording of the employee's contract). There are substantial human rights implications in carrying out alcohol/drug screening on individuals. Such testing will constitute an invasion of privacy under Article 8 of the Human Rights Act 1998, and will be justified only if:

- The screening is conducted in order to achieve a clearly identified, legitimate aim.

- The type of screening deployed is appropriate and necessary in order to achieve that aim.

- The screening programme is not excessive in its scope or content in relation to the aim to be achieved.

Thus screening conducted to ensure safety in the workplace (where the employees' jobs are safety-sensitive) would be potentially justifiable, while blanket screening of all employees irrespective of the jobs they carry out would be excessive and thus not justifiable under human rights principles.

Because the Human Rights Act 1998 is concerned with the rights of individuals as against the state, only public sector employers are directly affected by its provisions. However, private sector employers are affected indirectly on account of a provision in the Act that obliges courts and tribunals (as public authorities themselves) to interpret all existing legislation, including employment law, in such a way as is compatible with the Act insofar as is reasonably practicable. This could mean, for example, that a private sector employee whose Article 8 rights were breached by an employer could cite this in a claim for unfair dismissal. The result could be that the tribunal would rule that the employer had acted unreasonably in breaching the individual's right to privacy, the net result being a ruling that the dismissal was unfair on grounds of unreasonableness. Thus an employee dismissed for refusing to undergo alcohol or drug screening where there was no legitimate reason to screen him or her in the first place, and in circumstances where there were no safety implications at stake, could well succeed in a claim for unfair dismissal, irrespective of the employer's policy and rules on screening.

Data protection implications

Screening employees for alcohol consumption or use of drugs would also engage the provisions of the Data Protection Act 1998, since a record would inevitably be created of the results of any screening.

Under the Data Protection Act 1998, information about someone's physical or mental health is regarded as 'sensitive data', which means (among other things) that the employer must in most cases obtain the individual's express written consent before the information can be obtained or held on record.

Furthermore, the Employment Practices Data Protection Code, Part 4: Information about Workers' Health makes the following points in relation to drugs and alcohol testing:

- Employers should carry out an impact assessment in order to determine whether alcohol and/or drug screening is justified.

- The collection of information via alcohol and drug testing is unlikely to be justified unless it is for health and safety reasons and the type of testing applied addresses an identifiable risk.

- Testing should be confined to staff who are employed to work in safety-critical activities rather than being applied in blanket fashion to all workers in the business.

- The testing of all employees in a business will not be justified if only those engaged in particular activities could pose a risk.

- The amount of personal information obtained and held as a result of alcohol or drug testing should be kept to a minimum, for example by using tests that detect only recent exposure to the substances being tested for.

- Employers who conduct testing should use the least intrusive method possible to achieve their objectives.

- Employers should consider using tests of cognitive ability, rather than alcohol or drug screening, as such methods do not involve any invasive medical procedures.

- Testing should be carried out only for substances that are likely to have a significant bearing on employees' work.

- Testing should be designed to reflect the extent of exposure that is likely to have a significant bearing on employees' employment, for example an amount of alcohol above that used by the police when breath-testing drivers.

- The criteria used for selection for testing should be properly documented, adhered to and communicated to all affected employees.

- Testing should normally be designed to detect impairment at work, rather than illegal use of substances in an employee's private life.

- Employers should ensure that all staff are informed that drug or alcohol testing is taking place, and know the possible consequences of being tested.

- Testing should be carried out only by suitably qualified and competent personnel, and should be subject to rigorous control procedures.

The employee will have the same right to confidentiality as any other employee with a serious medical condition.

How to introduce a drug/alcohol screening policy fairly

For employers who decide to introduce a drug/alcohol screening policy, the aim should be to introduce a system that will serve the dual purpose of protecting the health and safety of the workforce and supporting staff who may have an alcohol or drug-related problem.

The introduction of a new policy of this type will, however, require consultation and agreement with the workforce or their representatives. This is because the introduction of a new procedure with such major implications would constitute a variation to contracts of employment, and changes to contractual terms cannot be brought about unilaterally. There are also human rights and data protection implications (see above under 'Human rights implications of screening policies' and 'Data protection implications').

To proceed in an over-hasty manner without employees' agreement may give rise to claims for breach of contract or constructive dismissal. A full programme of consultation should be undertaken, with plenty of time allocated to consider fully the views of the staff to whom the policy, if approved, would apply. Employees should subsequently be given a minimum of three months' notice of the introduction of the policy.

When devising a policy on screening, the employer should consider carefully to whom it should be applied. As stated above under 'Human rights implications of screening policies', it would not be appropriate to screen employees in a blanket fashion irrespective of whether there was any legitimate business reason for doing so. A desire to treat staff consistently will not, on its own, qualify as justification for blanket screening. However, having decided which employees are to be screened (depending on the jobs they perform and any safety implications), any screening policy should be applied to all staff in that category and there should be no exemptions on grounds of seniority.

It will also be vital to ensure clear communication of the policy, the way in which it will work, the reasons for it, and the consequences if an employee tests positive. It will be equally important to make it clear what will happen if someone refuses without good reason to submit to a test (that is, whether this will be regarded as gross misconduct and lead to dismissal).

It will also be vital, if random testing is to be carried out, to ensure that the system used to select candidates for screening is genuinely random: that candidates are selected in an unpredictable way, and that the selection process is properly monitored.

Ensuring alcohol/drug testing is properly carried out

Alcohol and drug testing must, of course, be carried out by personnel who are fully qualified and trained. Employers should carefully monitor this and insist on evidence that tests are being correctly carried out in accordance with laid-down procedures. In particular, they should ensure that:

- Testing is carried out in a sensitive and private manner with due regard to the employee's dignity.

- Testing is done in a way that ensures the least possible intrusion into privacy.

- The results of testing are fully discussed with the individual prior to the test result being made available to the employer.

- The results of all tests are kept absolutely secure and confidential with proper security measures in place, including measures to restrict access to authorised personnel only.

How to deal with a positive test result: support/rehabilitation or dismissal?

Employers, when devising an alcohol/drug screening programme, need to decide as a matter of policy how they will deal with an employee who tests positive for alcohol or drugs. There are two broad approaches:

- to state in the policy that someone who tests positive will be offered support and will not, in the case of a first positive test result, be subjected to disciplinary action (see above under 'Offering support where the employee is thought to have an addiction'), or

- to make it clear than any positive test result will provide grounds for disciplinary action, up to and including summary dismissal.

Which approach is appropriate will depend on the nature of the employer's business and the safety issues involved. Equally, each case will need to be viewed on its own facts. It is important to understand that, irrespective of the wording of the employer's policy, the dismissal of an employee who tests positive for an illegal substance will not automatically be fair. The fairness or otherwise of a dismissal will always depend on the overall question of whether the employer has acted reasonably in all the circumstances of the individual case, taking into account any mitigating factors.

Much depends on the employer's original reasons for introducing the screening programme. If the prime reason behind the programme is to protect employees' health, offering support with a view to rehabilitation would be the logical approach. This approach could be combined with a rule that an employee who has tested positive will be required to undergo further testing at specified future intervals for a specified period of time. Any refusal on his or her part to accept the support offered, or any further positive test result within the specified time period, could then be regarded as misconduct leading to dismissal.

Alternatively, the employer may take the view that, for safety reasons, any positive test result should be cause for dismissal.

POINTS TO NOTE

- If an employee is an alcoholic or has become addicted to a particular drug, it is important to treat that person according to the same principles as would be applied to any other staff suffering from serious illness that affected their work.

- Disciplinary action is not normally appropriate if an employee has an alcohol or drugs-addiction and is therefore ill.

- Manifestations of an employee's alcohol problem that take the form of gross misconduct such as violence at work may be treated as such, depending on the circumstances of the particular case.

- If an employee has admitted to having a problem linked to alcohol or drugs, a course of action leading potentially to rehabilitation should be discussed with a view to agreeing the way ahead.

- A programme of rehabilitation may involve the offer of time off work for the employee to undergo an agreed course of medical treatment and/or counselling, and/or the offer of reduced hours or lighter work for a temporary period.

- Whether it is reasonable for the employer to regard being under the influence of alcohol at work as gross misconduct justifying summary dismissal will depend on all the circumstances of the individual case.

- If there are grounds to believe that an employee is under the influence of alcohol at work, it will usually be appropriate initially to suspend the employee from work on full pay.

- It will not normally be appropriate for an employer to impose rules on employees' use of alcohol in their own private time except in certain defined circumstances, for example during on-call periods.

- Employers will be committing a criminal offence under the Misuse of Drugs Act 1971 if they know that illegal drugs are being kept, supplied or used on their premises.

- Recreational use of drugs outside work may or may not constitute grounds for disciplinary action, depending on the employer's policies and rules (if any) and on whether there is likely to be any adverse impact on the employee's performance, conduct or attendance as a consequence of the drugs.

- A ban on employees taking drugs in their own private time would constitute an invasion of the right to a private life under Article 8 of the Human Rights Act 1998, although the right to privacy may be legitimately restricted in certain defined circumstances.

- Criminal offences, for example drugs dealing, committed outside work may give rise to fair dismissal, but only if there is a connection between the employee's leisure-time conduct and his or her employment.

- The key criterion when considering whether it is appropriate to implement alcohol/drug screening, is whether an employee's use of alcohol or drugs would be likely to create a safety risk in the workplace.

- Alcohol/drug testing of all employees in a business will not be justified if only those engaged in particular activities could pose a risk.

ACTION POINTS

- Try to establish, if an employee has an alcohol or drug-related problem, whether this is caused by the addiction (in which case the person should be regarded as 'sick') or whether the behaviour represents misconduct.

- Make it clear in writing at the outset of any rehabilitation programme that continued support and sympathetic treatment will depend on the employee following through any course of medical treatment that has been agreed.

- Seek expert medical advice on the employee's condition if alcohol or drugs use is suspected, ideally by arranging for him or her to be interviewed and examined by an occupational doctor.

- Agree not to institute (or to discontinue) disciplinary action against an employee who is an alcoholic or drug addict provided he or she is willing to cooperate with the employer to work towards rehabilitation.

- Ensure there is a statement in the employer's disciplinary code or rules that no employee is permitted to have alcohol in his or her personal possession at the workplace, or to consume alcohol during working hours, and that any breach of these rules will be regarded as gross misconduct.

- Refrain from making uninformed assumptions about an employee who appears to be under the influence of alcohol at work since the person may, for example, be taking prescribed medication that has side effects.

- Consider whether to impose rules banning the consumption of alcohol during periods in which employees are on call, especially if a call out would involve a requirement for the employee to drive.

- Devise and implement clear rules that ban employees from consuming illegal drugs in their own time only if impaired performance could lead to a safety risk in the workplace.

- Extend any policy governing alcohol and drug use to work-related functions, making it clear that possession of an illegal substance or over-indulgence in alcohol at such a function will be regarded as gross misconduct.

- Ensure that the purpose of any alcohol/drug screening programme is to assess the competence of an employee to perform a specific job, and not a way of controlling off-duty behaviour where the employee's work is not likely to be affected.

- Recognise that there are substantial human rights implications in carrying out alcohol/drug screening on individuals and that such testing will be justified only if (a) the screening is conducted in order to achieve a clearly identified legitimate aim, and (b) the type of screening deployed is not excessive but is appropriate and necessary in order to achieve that aim.

- Carry out an impact assessment in order to determine whether alcohol and/or drug screening is justified.

- Confine alcohol/drug screening to employees whose activities have a significant impact on health and safety rather than applying the screening in blanket fashion to all workers in the business.

- Monitor any alcohol/drug screening carefully, and insist on evidence that tests are being correctly carried out in accordance with laid-down procedures and that testing is done in a way that ensures the least possible intrusion into employees' privacy.

CHAPTER 6

SMOKING AT WORK

Introduction

Much has been said and written over the last two decades about the health risks of smoking, and the harmful effects of passive smoking. Most workplaces nowadays have smoking policies, and many have an outright ban on smoking inside the employer's premises. It was reported in *People Management* in December 2004 that some employers are refusing to recruit people who smoke on the grounds that they are more likely than non-smokers to be off sick, are less productive than non-smokers due to time off for smoking breaks, and may cause damage to the fabric of the workplace.

The government has announced that smoking in most workplaces will be banned completely by 2008. This means that smoking rooms will no longer be permitted and, employees who wish to smoke during the working day will be forced to go outside during their breaks. The Scottish Parliament has confirmed that smoking will be banned in all workplaces and public places in Scotland, including licensed premises, as from the spring of 2006.

Attitudes towards smoking have changed considerably over the past 10 years or so. There is a much greater awareness nowadays of the health risks inherent in smoking and of the risks to non-smokers from inhaling other people's tobacco smoke. This in turn makes it more difficult than in the past for employers to defend a decision not to put smoking restrictions in place within their workplaces.

This chapter discusses the issue of smoking at work from the perspective of employees' health and wellbeing, and explains how to introduce and manage a smoking policy. Further information can be obtained from the Health and Safety Executive (HSE), for example from their booklet titled *Passive Smoking at Work*, available on their website: www.hse.gov.uk.

Legal issues associated with smoking

There are a number of legal provisions to consider when imposing rules on smoking at work. The main issues are:

- Duties under health and safety legislation. These oblige employers to take care of the health, safety and welfare at work of all their workers.

- The employer's common law duty to safeguard employees' health. An employer who declines to introduce smoking restrictions in the workplace is leaving itself open to claims of personal injury by employees who develop an illness as result of passive smoking.

- The employer's implied duty to provide and monitor for staff a working environment which is reasonably suitable for the performance of their duties.

- Employees' contractual rights. The introduction of a smoking policy or a smoking ban without proper consultation could give rise to claims of constructive dismissal based on alleged breach of contract from those who wish to continue to smoke while at work.

- Unfair dismissal law. Employers may face unfair dismissal claims from employees with one year's service or more who are dismissed for breaching the company's rules on smoking at work.

When considering what type of policy to adopt in relation to smoking, employers have a number of options:

- to operate without any smoking restrictions in the workplace

- to introduce smoking restrictions only in specific areas of the workplace, such as areas where there might be a fire risk, or where food is handled

- to segregate smokers and non-smokers into separate work areas, banning smoking in open-plan areas

- to introduce a general smoking ban in all parts of the employer's premises, but provide an enclosed smoking room or set area for those who wish to smoke during breaks

- to introduce a complete smoking ban throughout the workplace, perhaps extending it to company cars, the company car park and/or the area immediately outside the workplace.

It has become commonplace for employers to implement a complete ban on smoking at work, principally out of concerns over the detrimental effects of passive smoking on employees' health and wellbeing.

Health and safety implications of permitting smoking in the workplace

There are a number of legislative measures in place that bear on smoking at work, and also common law duties imposed by courts and tribunals.

Health and safety legislation

The Health and Safety at Work Act 1974 places a general duty on every employer to 'ensure, so far as is reasonably practicable, the health, safety and welfare at work of all his employees'. According to the Health and Safety Executive (HSE), this principle would apply to smoking at work and its effects. The HSE states that 'passive smoking may be relevant to the welfare, and subject to medical evidence, the health of people at work'.

This means, in effect, that if there was evidence that a worker's health was being put at risk by other people's tobacco smoke, for example if a particular worker had a respiratory condition that could be aggravated by passive smoking, then the employer would be under a duty to take appropriate steps to remove that risk to the employee's health.

Furthermore, the Management of Health and Safety at Work Regulations 1992 made it compulsory for employers to carry out risk assessments with regard to health and safety in the workplace. Under these regulations, employers have a duty to identify and assess any risks to employees' health and safety, and to determine and put in place appropriate measures to prevent or reduce these risks. It seems likely that these obligations would incorporate the duty to assess the risk to health from the effects of passive smoking in the workplace.

Useful guidance on how to carry out a risk assessment is available in the HSE publication *Five Steps to Risk Assessment*.

Rest facilities

The Workplace (Health, Safety and Welfare) Regulations 1992 set out provisions obliging employers to provide suitable rest facilities for all their workers. Under the regulations, employers are under a duty to provide rest areas, and make arrangements whereby non-smokers may use rest rooms or rest areas without suffering discomfort from tobacco smoke. The regulations also require employers to make 'effective and suitable provision to ensure that every enclosed workplace is ventilated by a sufficient quantity of fresh or purified air'. Doing nothing to prevent the workplace being contaminated with cigarette smoke could arguably contravene this aspect of the regulations.

The Health and Safety Executive's stance

The Health and Safety Executive's booklet, *Passive Smoking at Work*, recommends that employers should:

- if smoking is permitted at all, segregate smokers from non-smokers

- make provision to protect non-smokers from discomfort caused by tobacco smoke in rest rooms and rest areas

- introduce a specific policy on smoking in the workplace that should give priority to the needs of non-smokers who do not wish to breathe tobacco smoke

- regard non-smoking as the norm in enclosed workplaces

- consult staff fully before introducing a smoking policy and take time to develop the policy

- take special care of people who have a health condition that may be made worse by tobacco smoke.

The Health and Safety Commission is committed to introducing an approved Code of Practice dealing with passive smoking at work, which at the time of writing is in draft form and is being revised. The Code, once implemented, will require employers to take all reasonably practical steps to protect employees from the effects of passive smoking at work.

Although the Code will not be legally binding, as with other codes of practice its provisions may be taken into account in any proceedings before a court or employment tribunal. This means in effect that any failure to follow the recommendations contained in the Code will be likely to he held against the employer.

Common law duties

Over and above the provisions contained in health and safety legislation, employers are under a common law duty to take reasonable care to protect the health and welfare of all their employees. Given the mass of clear evidence of the harmful effects of passive smoking, it could be argued that a refusal to consider implementing (or a failure to properly implement) smoking restrictions in the workplace could be a breach of that common law duty. The effect of this could be that employees who were genuinely worried that their health was at risk, for example if they worked in an area where others smoked heavily, could resign and claim unfair constructive dismissal (subject to their having a minimum of one year's continuous service with the employer).

The implied duty to provide a suitable working environment for employees

Many implied rights in employment come about as a result of court and tribunal decisions. One such right was created by the EAT in 1997 following a claim from an employee who had resigned on account of her employer's failure to deal with workplace tobacco smoke. The case, *Waltons & Morse v Dorrington [1997] IRLR 488*, created the implied duty on employers to provide and monitor a working environment which is reasonably tolerable and suitable for employees to perform their duties (see 'Key case 1' in the box below).

Key case 1

Waltons & Morse v Dorrington [1997] IRLR 488

Ms Dorrington, who was a non-smoker, had worked as a secretary for a firm of solicitors for eight years when she was moved to an open-plan area. She experienced discomfort due to the presence of cigarette smoke caused by the fact that four of the other secretaries smoked regularly, and also that colleagues who occupied nearby offices smoked heavily. When Ms Dorrington raised the matter initially with management, a policy was introduced banning smoking in the open-plan area. This did not, however, solve the problem for Ms Dorrington because smoke from a nearby smoking room and from the private offices still wafted through to the open-plan area where she worked. She raised the matter with management again, but was ultimately told that she would just have to put up with it. She subsequently resigned and claimed constructive dismissal.

The employment tribunal found from the evidence that the air quality had been intolerable for a non-smoker and that the employers were in breach of an implied term that the employer should provide a reasonably suitable and tolerable working environment for employees to perform their duties. Thus there had been a breach of contract entitling Ms Dorrington to resign. The employer appealed to the EAT, who rejected the appeal and upheld Ms Dorrington's complaint.

The tribunal also expressed the view that it is not sufficient for an employer to try to balance the interests of smokers with non-smokers so that each is accommodated equally. They commented that the choice of an individual not to smoke does not have a detrimental impact on those nearby, while the reverse is not the case. They stated that 'It is neither fair nor accurate to describe the curbing of freedom to smoke as treating the non-smoker more favourably'.

The key principle from the *Dorrington* case is that an employer's failure to provide a working environment that is reasonably free from cigarette smoke may constitute a breach of contract entitling any individual who finds the situation intolerable to resign and claim constructive dismissal (subject to the employee having a minimum of one year's continuous service). Another interesting outcome is the effect of the tribunal's observations on the issue of balancing the interests of smokers with those of non-smokers. The practical effect of these observations is that an employer who attempts in good faith to accommodate employees who wish to smoke at work may inadvertently breach the implied employment rights of non-smokers.

This does not mean that employers are compelled to operate a complete smoking ban in the workplace. The implied duty is to provide a 'reasonably suitable' working environment for employees and this aim may be capable of being achieved satisfactorily by the provision of an effective air ventilation system. So long as the ventilation system is efficient enough to remove most of the tobacco smoke, and so long as smoke is not allowed to waft through from other areas, the duty to provide a reasonably suitable working environment for the employees to perform their duties would be satisfied.

In contrast, a smoking policy that resulted in smoke drifting through to non-smoking areas would leave it open for employees who suffered discomfort as a result to claim that the employer had breached their contracts.

Workplaces where customers smoke: the implications

The government has confirmed that it will implement a ban on smoking in most workplaces by 2008 in order to protect the health of the nation. Licensed premises that do not sell food will, however, be exempt from the ban. The Scottish Parliament has gone one step further by announcing that smoking will be banned in all workplaces and public places in Scotland, including licensed premises, as from the spring of 2006. This reflects growing evidence that measures such as increased ventilation and the provision of no-smoking areas taken by restaurants, pubs and other venues do not prevent exposure to smoke and have only a minimal effect. Some ventilation systems allow discharged air to be re-circulated, and unless the air from smoking areas is discharged separately the re-circulated air is likely to be contaminated by tobacco smoke.

The ban on smoking in public places will inevitably have a major impact on employers in certain industries, in particular hotels, restaurants and bars, and also in residential and nursing homes where the residents smoke. A discussion about the effects of such a ban on trade is outside the scope of this book, but there is no doubt that a ban would be of great benefit to the health and wellbeing of people who are employed in industries where their customers or clients are (as at present) permitted to smoke on the premises.

Smoking policies

It is commonplace nowadays for employers either to operate smoking policies that ban smoking completely, or apply a ban to certain areas with other areas being designated as smoking zones. Some smokers perceive such rules as discrimination, but whatever terminology is used, 'discrimination' against smokers in the form of a smoking ban, partial or total, is not unlawful. Equally, it is not unlawful to refuse to employ someone on the grounds that they smoke, nor to ask questions at a selection interview related to the job applicant's smoking habits.

In its booklet *Passive Smoking at Work*, the HSE recommends that all employers should introduce a policy to control smoking in the workplace. It points out that passive smoking can and does cause acute physical distress for non-smokers in a number of ways, for example irritation of the eyes, throat and respiratory tract.

Right to smoke?

It is important to recognise that there is no such thing as a 'right to smoke' at work. This principle was clearly established in the case of *Dryden v Greater Glasgow Health Board 1992 IRLR 469* (see 'Key case 2' in the box below).

Key case 2

Dryden v Greater Glasgow Health Board 1992 IRLR 469

The employer in this case (the Health Board) had previously operated a policy that permitted smoking in certain designated areas of its hospitals, although smoking was banned in the public areas. With the aim of strengthening its no-smoking policy, the Board proposed to introduce a total no-smoking ban. With this in mind, the Board consulted various trade unions and staff interest groups within their hospitals. They also offered assistance, including counselling, to any employees who wished to stop smoking or who believed that the outright ban would cause them problems, and gave over three months notice of the introduction of the new policy.

The employee, Ms Dryden, who was a nursing auxiliary working in operating theatres, was a heavy smoker and despite the provision of help, failed to quit smoking prior to the ban being implemented. The effect of the ban on her was that she no longer had access to a smoking area during her breaks. Within only a few days of the ban being implemented, she found the situation intolerable and resigned. She subsequently brought a claim for constructive dismissal to an employment tribunal, arguing that the Health Board had breached her contract of employment by introducing the smoking ban. This was based on her allegation that she had the implied right to smoke at work.

The tribunal, however, rejected Ms Dryden's arguments outright. They held that there was neither an express, nor an implied term in her contract of employment entitling her to smoke at work. They went on to say that a right to smoke would in any event be an inappropriate term to imply into an employment contract.

> When the case was appealed, the EAT made observations on the contractual implications where an employer introduces a new policy, and stated that a policy that has a legitimate purpose and is introduced in a reasonable manner would be unlikely to give rise to the constructive dismissal of any employee who could not, due to personal factors, comply with the policy. Ms Dryden failed to have the tribunal's decision overturned on appeal.

It is clear from the *Dryden* case that employers are free to decide whether or not to introduce a no-smoking policy. Equally clear is the principle that an employer must proceed in an objective and reasonable manner when proposing to introduce a no-smoking policy or smoking restrictions in the workplace. The *Dryden* decision does not pave the way for employers to act arbitrarily or unilaterally in introducing a new policy or rules that will change the way employees work or affect their welfare at work. On the contrary, care, patience and consideration must be exercised in introducing such a policy.

How to introduce a smoking policy fairly

The initial introduction of a smoking policy or smoking restrictions at work raises an emotive issue and is likely to produce different reactions from different people. It may of course create resistance and resentment among employees who have always been allowed to smoke at work. It is therefore in the interests of employers and employees alike to ensure that general cooperation is gained prior to the implementation of any new rules on smoking, and the employer should adopt a sympathetic and patient approach, especially if proposing to ban smoking in areas where it has not previously been restricted.

The introduction of any new policy, procedure or set of rules that is likely to affect employees at work will constitute a variation to individuals' contracts of employment. It is well established that changes to contractual terms cannot be brought about unilaterally, but may only be implemented with the agreement of both parties. It follows that the employer will need to take steps to gain employees' agreement to the proposed changes. To proceed in an over-hasty manner without agreement may give rise to claims for unfair constructive dismissal, based on the argument that the actions of the employer amounted to a breach of the implied duty of mutual trust and confidence.

To introduce new rules on smoking therefore, the employer should proceed as follows:

- Set out the proposed new policy and rules in writing.

- Ensure the proposed policy and rules are appropriate to the workplace, taking all circumstances into account.

- Commence a programme of consultation with employees, either directly or through trade unions or workforce representatives.

- Explain fully the employer's proposal to introduce a smoking ban or smoking restrictions, and the reason why such a change is felt to be appropriate.

- Invite employees or their representatives to provide feedback on the proposals.

- Take on board any concerns and objections put forward by employees and consider whether they can be accommodated.

- Take reasonable steps to accommodate employees' concerns; for example, consider offering support to staff who wish to give up smoking.

- Follow up all consultations in writing.

- Once proposals have been modified in the light of any reasonable suggestions or objections from employees, give individual written notice to all staff of the company's decision to introduce the smoking policy and rules at a specified future date.

- Ensure the notice period is reasonable; for example, three months notice would be likely to be viewed as reasonable by an employment tribunal.

- Consider whether it would be helpful to implement the policy with a transitional period during which a more lenient approach will be taken, for example towards employees who have difficulty complying fully with new no-smoking rules.

- Amend disciplinary procedures to take account of the new smoking policy in order to make it clear to all staff what the penalty will be for any breach of the rules.

Key points for the employer to bear in mind are that:

- The policy should be designed to give priority to the needs of non-smokers in order to protect them from the discomfort and possible ill-effects of breathing in other people's tobacco smoke.

- On no account should the employer try to rush through the introduction of a new smoking policy.

- Employers should take great care to ensure every employee is informed individually of the new rules and their implications; a notice placed on the notice board will not be sufficient.

- The prospective sanctions for employees who breach smoking rules should be made absolutely clear; if the penalty is to be dismissal, for example, this should be spelled out in unambiguous language.

If employers fail to follow through a genuine process of consultation prior to the introduction of a smoking policy, they leave themselves at risk of resignations followed by claims for unfair constructive dismissal. Furthermore, if the policy is not introduced in a fair and reasonable manner with the consent of the workforce, any subsequent dismissal of an employee who flouts the new smoking rules would be likely to be ruled unfair by an employment tribunal.

Model policy on smoking

Employers may wish to adopt a policy similar to the one in the box below, adapted to suit the individual workplace where necessary.

Complete ban or designated smoking areas?

There is no legal requirement for employers to provide smoking facilities for employees, or to permit them to smoke in, for example, the company car park. The provision of smoking facilities is a general management issue and will depend on the employer's approach to the question of employee health, available space and general opinion within the company.

If the employer elects to provide inside areas in which employees are permitted to smoke during their breaks, it should ensure that the smoking areas are effectively screened so that smoke cannot waft through to other areas, thus affecting employees at work. It will be equally important to ensure that an efficient ventilation system is put in place. The ventilation system should be designed so that either the air from smoking areas and that from non-smoking areas is discharged separately (so that the air from smoking areas is not allowed to re-circulate) or the discharged air is properly decontaminated before it re-enters the system.

If the decision is to introduce a complete smoking ban, the employer will have to decide whether to apply the ban to all company property including car parks and other outside areas belonging to the employer, for example any garden area, the pavement immediately outside the office building, and of course company vehicles.

Enforcing the policy

It is very important for all employers with smoking policies to ensure that they fully and clearly inform their employees not only of the policy itself, but also what the penalty will be for breaches of smoking rules. If smoking in unauthorised areas is to be regarded as gross misconduct and the penalty is to be dismissal, then this must be

Model policy on smoking

The Company holds the view that smoking, including passive smoking, constitutes an unacceptable risk to employees' health and welfare. All employers are under a statutory duty to take care of employees' health, safety and welfare at work. In order to comply with that duty, and in order to prevent tobacco smoke from causing discomfort to non-smokers, the Company has implemented a smoking policy. The Company considers that it is in the interests of all staff that the working environment should be free from tobacco smoke.

The policy takes the form of a complete smoking ban in all parts of the Company's premises [including the car park, garden grounds and inside all company vehicles]. [Employees are also forbidden to smoke in the public area immediately outside the Company's premises]. This in effect, means that the Company adopts a zero-tolerance approach to smoking.

[Alternative clause]

The policy takes the form of a smoking ban inside the Company's premises. The Company has, however, made a rest area available in [state location] which may be used as a smoking room during designated lunch [and tea] breaks. Employees who smoke are expected to do so only in the designated area and only during their permitted breaks. The Company will not permit smokers to take additional breaks over and above the designated lunch [and tea] breaks.

This policy applies to all staff, whether permanent or temporary, including sub-contractors' and agency personnel who are working on the premises. Visitors to the Company, including job applicants, should be informed of the policy and asked to comply with it.

Employees who breach the Company's smoking policy by smoking on Company premises [except in the designated area during permitted breaks] will be subject to disciplinary action.

A first offence will give rise to a final written warning, while a repeat offence will result in summary dismissal. [Alternative clause] Any instance of smoking on Company premises [except in the designated area during permitted breaks], including a first offence, will be regarded as gross misconduct with the result that the employee will be summarily dismissed from the Company.

Employees who are smokers and who would like help to give up the habit may, if they wish, contact [name of suitable individual, e.g. an occupational nurse or HR officer] who will provide information and appropriate sources where help may be obtained.

intimated in an unambiguous way. If an employee is dismissed for breach of smoking rules and can demonstrate that he or she had not been clearly informed that such a breach would result in dismissal, the dismissal will in all likelihood be deemed unfair.

It will also be important to apply the policy and rules consistently. If smoking is condoned in some areas despite a ban, or if smoking rules are sometimes overlooked at management's discretion, then employees may genuinely come to believe that smoking at work is not regarded as serious misconduct. In these circumstances, any dismissal of an employee for smoking at work would be viewed as unfair by an employment tribunal.

Although employment tribunals have been willing in general to rule that dismissals for smoking offences are fair where clear rules are in place banning smoking (assuming also that the rules have been fully communicated), it will nevertheless be essential for an employer to view the facts of each case individually before taking any decision to dismiss anyone who has transgressed the rules. No matter how clear it is that an employer has grounds to dismiss an employee, the employer is also under a statutory duty to act reasonably; that is, ensure that dismissal for the stated reason is a reasonable response under all the circumstances. Reasonableness will also involve carrying out a full and fair procedure. This in turn will include:

- a thorough investigation into the circumstances of the case

- notifying the employee in writing of the case against him or her

- giving the employee the opportunity to state his or her version of events at an interview (at which he or she will have the right to be accompanied by a colleague or trade union representative)

- considering any mitigating factors

- allowing a right of appeal against any decision to dismiss.

Smoking breaks and their implications, both for smokers and their non-smoking colleagues

The sight of clusters of workers huddled in workplace doorways smoking cigarettes is a common one nowadays. There are a number of possible implications associated with this:

- There may be a negative effect on the organisation's image if employees are regularly seen by customers and clients smoking outside the building.

- The time spent by employees taking smoking breaks may become a problem.

- There may be an adverse impact on non-smoking employees if their colleagues leave their work stations regularly to take smoking breaks.

Many organisations that have banned smoking inside their workplaces have created a new problem for themselves in that staff who smoke are more frequently absent from their desks than their non-smoking colleagues. Non-smoking employees may well feel a legitimate sense of grievance if other staff take what they perceive to be excessive and illegitimate breaks from work. They may even become disillusioned and resentful if their colleagues are seemingly permitted to take unlimited smoking breaks while they continue to work normally.

This is, of course, a management issue rather than a legal one, and ideally it is an issue that should be addressed at the time any new or revised smoking policy is implemented. Clear rules or guidelines on breaks from work may need to be specified, for example:

- whether smoking breaks are permitted at all over and above any existing breaks (e.g. in addition to an existing lunch break or official tea break)

- if smoking breaks are permitted, how many are allowed, when they may or may not be taken, and the maximum length of each break

- if breaks are permitted, that all staff are entitled to them; in other words, non-smoking employees may also take the breaks, for example to enjoy a cup of coffee.

If, despite guidelines being issued, some employees take breaks that are excessive either in number or in duration, it may be necessary to re-emphasise the company's rules on taking breaks from work. Any employee who continues to flout the rules would then be dealt with under the employer's normal disciplinary procedure.

POINTS TO NOTE

- Smoking in most workplaces is to be banned in England and Wales by 2008, and in all workplaces in Scotland by 2006.

- There are a number of legal provisions to consider when imposing rules on smoking at work, including health and safety legislation, common law duties, employees' contractual rights and unfair dismissal law.

- Under health and safety legislation, if there was evidence that a worker's health was being put at risk by other people's tobacco smoke, the employer would be under a duty to take appropriate steps to remove that risk to the employee's health.

- An employer's failure to provide a working environment that is reasonably free from cigarette smoke may constitute a breach of contract, entitling an employee who finds the situation intolerable to resign and claim constructive dismissal.

- There is no such thing as a 'right to smoke' at work.

- It is in the interests of both employers and employees to ensure that general cooperation is gained prior to the implementation of any new rules on smoking.

- If employers fail to engage in a genuine process of consultation prior to the introduction of a smoking policy, they will leave themselves at risk of claims for unfair constructive dismissal.

- There is no legal requirement for employers to provide smoking facilities for employees, nor to permit them to smoke in, for example, the company car park.

- It is very important for all employers with smoking policies to ensure that they fully and clearly inform their employees not only of the policy itself, but also what the penalty will be for breaches of the rules.

- The question of whether employees are granted smoking breaks, and the number and duration of any such breaks, is a management issue that should ideally be clarified at the time any smoking policy is introduced.

ACTION POINTS

- Introduce a specific policy on smoking in the workplace that gives priority to the needs of non-smokers in order to protect them from the discomfort and possible ill-effects of breathing in other people's tobacco smoke.

- Be aware that employees who are genuinely worried that their health is being put at risk, for example if they work in an area where others smoke heavily, could resign and claim unfair constructive dismissal.

- Proceed in an objective and reasonable manner when proposing to introduce a no-smoking policy or smoking restrictions in the workplace.

- Consult employees fully, either directly or through trade unions or workforce representatives, before finalising any proposals to implement a smoking policy or smoking rules.

- Give reasonable notice (for example three months) of the introduction of a new or revised smoking policy.

- Take great care to ensure every employee is informed individually of any new smoking rules and their implications.

- Amend disciplinary procedures to take account of any new smoking rules in order to make it absolutely clear what the penalties will be for any breach of the rules.

- Make sure that any designated smoking areas are effectively screened so that smoke cannot waft through to other areas, thus adversely affecting employees at work.

- Review any instance where an employee has breached the employer's smoking policy carefully before taking any decision to dismiss the employee who has transgressed the rules.

- Recognise the fact that if employees are permitted to take unlimited smoking breaks, this may have an adverse impact on non-smoking employees who may resent their colleagues' frequent absences from their desks.

CHAPTER 7

DEALING WITH LONG-TERM ILL-HEALTH ABSENCE

Introduction

As part of an organisation's strategy to promote employees' health and wellbeing, it will be important to put in place effective policies and procedures to manage long-term ill-health absence. Although instances of long-term absence are less common than one-day sickness absences, long-term absence accounts for more than 30 per cent of all time lost to sickness in the United Kingdom. Clearly long-term absence can create difficulties for the employer and can also bring extra pressure to bear on the absent employee's colleagues, whose work may be disrupted or who may object if they are expected to take additional duties on board.

The key underlying objective of long-term ill-health management will be to achieve an acceptable and fair balance between the protection and promotion of staff health and wellbeing on the one hand and the needs of the business on the other.

This section aims to explore the topic of how to manage long-term ill-health absence effectively, and also tackles some sensitive topics such as AIDS, mental illness and the dismissal of an employee on the grounds of incapacity.

Managing long-term sickness absence

The effective management of long-term ill-health absence will benefit both the employer and their employees in a number of ways.

- Employees will be clear what their entitlements are in the event that they are absent from work as a result of long-term sickness.

- Line managers will understand their duties and responsibilities towards staff in the event of long-term sickness absence, and what role they are expected to play in supporting the employee.

- Employees will understand that their employer genuinely cares about staff who fall ill, and are therefore less likely to worry about the possible consequences of long-term absence.

- Employees are more likely to return to work sooner if they feel that their employer adopts a supportive attitude towards them.

- Employees who return to work after a period of sickness absence are more likely to be re-integrated quickly, and thus resume effective working at an earlier stage.

Policy issues

The starting point for the effective management of long-term ill-health absence is the creation of effective policies and procedures. The employer may wish to consider formulating the following:

- a policy statement outlining the employer's approach to long-term ill-health absence

- a policy on referral to occupational health specialists (see Chapter 8)

- a policy governing the process for termination of an employee's employment where that person has become incapacitated (see below under 'The last resort: dismissal').

The main theme of any ill-health absence policy should be that the employer will offer support to employees who are absent from work due to genuine sickness. The policy should:

- provide a definition of long-term sickness absence (typically any absence of four weeks or more)

- outline the employer's general approach towards long-term sickness absence

- explain clearly what occupational sick pay employees will be entitled to receive, the length of time sick pay will be payable and any conditions applicable to payment (see below under 'Paying sick pay')

- inform employees whether the employer operates a permanent health insurance scheme and how the scheme dovetails with occupational sick pay

- state whether the employer uses the services of an occupational doctor and describe the doctor's role in managing long-term ill-health absence

- clarify whether employees are obliged under the terms of their contracts to consent to be examined by an occupational doctor at the employer's request (which is to be recommended – see Chapter 8 under 'Using occupational doctors')

- specify who in the organisation will be responsible for communicating with the employee during periods of absence (see below under 'Communicating with the employee during periods of absence from work')

- state what measures will be adopted to facilitate the rehabilitation of an employee who has experienced long-term sickness (see below under 'Rehabilitating an employee who has been absent from work')

- outline the circumstances in which the employer will consider redeployment

- state whether the employer operates an ill-health retirement scheme, and if so, the terms of eligibility

- clarify whether and when the employer may consider the option of termination of an employee's contract on the grounds of long-term incapacity.

Model policy on long-term sickness absence

Employers may wish to adopt or adapt the model policy shown in the box below.

Model policy on long-term sickness absence

It is the policy of this Company to provide reasonable support to employees who are ill and medically certified as unfit to work. This statement outlines the Company's approach to long-term sickness absence (defined as any absence of four weeks or more due to illness or injury), the benefits that the employee is entitled to receive and what the Company will do to assist the employee's rehabilitation into the workplace once he or she recovers sufficiently to resume working.

The Company will pay an employee who is absent from work due to illness full basic salary for a period of [x weeks/months] followed by a period of [x weeks/months] on half basic pay. Payment of salary while off sick is conditional on the employee complying with the Company's rules on notification and certification, and on the employee consenting to be examined by an occupational doctor nominated by the Company at the request of the Company.

[The Company also operates a permanent health insurance scheme which is designed to provide an income to staff who are incapacitated for work for periods in excess of [   ] months. Full details of the scheme and its terms and

---

conditions are available from [ ]. The scheme has been set up so that benefit will commence at the time that entitlement to occupational sick pay expires in order to ensure that the employee continues to receive financial support during long-term sickness absence.

The Company retains the services of an occupational doctor. Employees are required under the terms of their contracts to agree to be examined by the doctor at the Company's request and to allow the doctor to provide a medical report to the Company. This will help the Company, in consultation with the employee, to make the best judgements regarding the employee's fitness to work, likely length of absence from work, the types of tasks that the employee may be able to undertake on return to work and any steps that the Company could take to facilitate the employee's return to work. The Company will meet all expenses associated with such medical examinations and reports.

During the employee's absence, the situation will be reviewed every [three/six] months with a view to determining whether any steps can be taken to support the employee and/or facilitate a return to work. The employee will be fully involved and consulted about these reviews. Furthermore, the employee's line manager will be responsible for maintaining contact with the employee and for arranging (with the employee's agreement) to visit the employee.

When an employee is ready to return to work after a period of long-term sickness absence, the Company will provide support in a number of ways. This will include providing an update for the employee on Company and departmental activities, agreeing any special arrangements in relation to hours of work and/or job duties, and offering general support to help the employee reintegrate quickly.

If the employee is fit to return to work, but unable to perform all the duties of his or her normal job, the Company will discuss any necessary adjustments with the employee. Adjustments may, for example, involve re-arranging job duties or offering the employee redeployment in another suitable job, on either a temporary or permanent basis.

[The Company operates an ill-health retirement scheme, details of which are available from [ ].

In the event that the employee is off sick for longer than [ ] (and if ill-health retirement is not an option), the Company may, from a business perspective, need to consider terminating the employee's employment. A decision to terminate will not, however, be taken lightly, and will only be made after full consultation with the employee and following medical recommendations from the Company's occupational doctor. Thus termination will be considered only as a last resort.

Communicating with the employee during periods of absence from work

Most people who are absent from work for a long period of time will appreciate being contacted on a regular basis by someone from the organisation. It is likely that an employee who is used to the social contact inherent in most workplaces will miss that contact and feel isolated. Telephone calls and/or visits from a line manager and from colleagues may represent a welcome link to 'normal life'. In contrast, if contact is not maintained with the employees who are absent, they may feel unwanted or undervalued and assume that their welfare is of no interest to the organisation.

Naturally, the employer should take care that any telephone calls or home visits do not create any unwanted pressure on the employee. The main aims of contact should be for the employer to:

- show interest and concern for the employee's health and wellbeing

- keep the employee informed as to developments in the organisation generally

- reassure the employee of the employer's ongoing support

- enable the employer to keep up to date with the employee's wellbeing and progress and (when appropriate) his or her prospective return to work

- (if appropriate) discuss the type of work the employee may be capable of performing on returning, and whether different (or part-time) work may be appropriate on either a temporary or permanent basis.

Employer policies on long-term sickness absence should specify who in the organisation is responsible for maintaining contact with the employee. Normally, this should be that person's line manager, although he or she may wish to delegate home visits (for example) to colleagues with whom the employee is friendly. Visits should always be arranged in advance at a time to suit the absent employee and should be undertaken only with his or her agreement. An alternative, if the employee prefers not to agree to home visits, would be to keep in touch by telephone, or even e-mail. The employee's views on how contact should be made should be sought and respected.

Paying sick pay

The question of whether an employer continues to pay an employee's normal wage or salary during periods when the employee is absent from work due to sickness is governed by the contract of employment. There is no statutory obligation on employers to continue normal pay. The employer must, however, include a clause in the employee's written terms of employment that specifies the employee's entitlements regarding the payment of sick pay and any conditions for eligibility for payment.

Although normal pay need not be continued, all employers are obliged to pay employees who are absent from work due to personal sickness prescribed amounts of statutory sick pay (SSP). At the time of writing, the prescribed rate of SSP is £66.15 per week (effective from April 2004). There is no minimum service requirement to qualify for SSP, and both full-time and part-time employees are eligible. However, employees who earn less than the equivalent of the lower national insurance earnings limit in force at the relevant time (£79.00 per week as from April 2004) are excluded. Where full salary is paid to an employee who is off sick, SSP must be offset against it (i.e. SSP must not be paid over and above normal pay).

Despite the absence of any statutory obligation to continue paying an employee's normal pay during periods of sickness absence, many employers choose to do so for specified periods of time. Such a policy can be very valuable to employees as it provides peace of mind and removes any need to worry about financial hardship in the event of sickness. An employee who is already ill will not be helped to recover by the burden of worry over how to cope financially.

A common policy is to offer full pay for a defined period of weeks or months (for example three months), followed by an equivalent period at half pay. Some employers grant employees enhancements to these benefits in line with their length of service.

Where it is the employer's policy to pay sick pay, it is advisable to include clauses in the policy document relating to sickness absence and sick pay to allow the employer to refuse to make payment in certain limited circumstances, which could include where:

- The employer has grounds to believe that the employee's sickness absence is not genuine (which grounds would need to be investigated and put to the employee in order to give an opportunity to answer the specific allegation).

- The employee fails to comply with the employer's contractual requirements regarding the provision of medical certificates or refuses without good reason to be examined by an occupational doctor.

- The number of separate occasions the employee has been absent within a specified period has exceeded a contractually agreed trigger point. Thus the employer is not compelled to pay sick pay repeatedly to someone who frequently goes off sick.

Consistency and fairness will be paramount in the management of sick pay, in particular if line managers are afforded a degree of discretion as to whether or not to authorise payments. If any element of the provision of sick pay is discretionary, there should be clear guidelines for line managers as to how they should exercise such discretion so that the matter is not left to chance.

Managing the effect on other employees of a colleague's absence

Often an employee's long-term absence causes operational difficulties. The work still has to be done, but the employer is deprived of the employee's knowledge and experience, possibly for a lengthy and undefined period.

If the employee's work cannot be covered by means of a temporary transfer into the job, or the recruitment of an agency temp to fill in, the employer may have to ask other staff in the same department (or possibly in other departments as well) to absorb elements of the employee's job until he or she returns to work.

Where this is the case, the matter should be carefully managed, and never just left to chance. The employer should:

- conduct a review of the employee's scope of work and workload to determine how it might be divided up

- hold a meeting with all relevant staff to consult them about how the absent employee's work is to be covered

- ask the staff for suggestions as to how the work could best be covered

- explain the importance of ensuring that the absent employee's work is properly covered during the absence

- taking into account the feedback received from staff, make decisions as to how the work should be reallocated

- ensure that, in redistributing the work, no employees are overloaded or required to take on duties that they are not fully trained to do, or capable of doing

- confirm the new arrangements in writing

- show appreciation to staff who agree to take additional work on board.

Rehabilitating an employee who has been absent from work

Just as it is important to manage an employee's long-term ill-health absence, it will be essential to carefully manage that person's return to work after a lengthy period away. Employers should take responsibility for making certain arrangements to support and facilitate a return to work. Managers should bear in mind that the employee may feel anxious about the prospect of returning, and worry about how to cope with the work and how he or she will be regarded by colleagues and by management (especially if the absence has been on account of a mental illness).

The employer should in the first instance arrange for a medical examination by an occupational doctor to double-check that the employee is genuinely able – both physically and mentally – to resume working. The doctor should be asked to comment on whether there are likely to be any residual health problems and also whether the employee will still be taking any medication after returning to work that might have side effects. For example, if someone will be taking medication that might cause tiredness (which may, in any event, be the case in the first few weeks after a return to work), the line manager should be made aware of the need to be tolerant and understanding. Another matter for an occupational doctor to comment on would be whether the employee should be exempted initially from any particular job duties, such as work that is particularly physically demanding or mentally stressful.

After taking medical advice, the employer should:

- consider, in consultation with the employee, and on the basis of the doctor's advice, whether any special arrangements need to be made for support in the initial stages, or whether any adjustment to his or her job duties would be advisable

- review, again in consultation with the employee and on the basis of the doctor's advice, whether it would be helpful for the employee to resume working initially on a part-time basis, which may ease the transition from a long stay at home to full-time working

- encourage the employee to make a social visit to the workplace shortly before resuming work so that he or she can have a chat with colleagues and be brought up to date on a range of matters

- arrange to meet with the employee (preferably before the return date, or if not, on the first day back at work) to discuss how he or she is feeling and what he or she feels capable (or not) of doing

- if the employee has been absent for a lengthy period of time, provide a 'mini-induction' to help with reintegration into the organisation, to give an update on company developments and departmental activities that have occurred during the period of absence, and to agree what support measures will be put in place and how progress will be monitored

- take positive steps to ensure that the employee feels that his or her return to work is welcomed and that management are supportive of this re-integration into the workplace

- consider appointing a 'mentor' or 'buddy' to support the employee in the first few weeks and deal with any general difficulties he or she may experience

- endeavour to give the employee meaningful work to do as soon as possible, to provide reassurance that he or she is valued and useful

- make sure the employee is not 'thrown into the deep end' by immediately being exposed to a huge backlog of work

- monitor the situation over the first few weeks after the employee's return to ensure he or she is coping with the workload and the day-to-day pressures inherent in the workplace.

Implications under the Disability Discrimination Act 1995

If an employee's long-term illness amounts to a disability in law, the employer will also have to adhere to the provisions of the Disability Discrimination Act 1995. An employee who has an illness that has lasted, or is likely to last, 12 months or more and that has a substantial adverse effect on their ability to carry out normal day-to-day activities will be protected by the Act.

Apart from the duty not to discriminate against someone on grounds of disability (or on grounds related to a disability), employers are obliged under the Act to make 'reasonable adjustments' to any provision, criterion or practice that they apply in order to accommodate the needs of a disabled employee. The duty kicks in if any of the employer's working policies procedures, practices or general arrangements would otherwise place the disabled employee at a substantial disadvantage. What is deemed to be a 'reasonable adjustment' will depend on a number of factors, including the size, resources and business demands of the organisation.

The most effective way to determine what is possible and reasonable will be to consult the employee, who after all will know more about the condition and its effects than anyone else.

The sorts of adjustments that might help an employee who has had a long-term illness could be to:

- allow the employee to take reasonable time off work with pay to attend medical appointments, therapy or other form of treatment

- alter the employee's job duties with the aim of exempting him or her from any tasks that would be difficult to perform under the circumstances, or that are particularly demanding

- allow the employee flexibility in the number of hours worked, at least initially

- permit more frequent or longer rest breaks for a period of time, for example if the employee's condition means that he or she tires easily

- agree that the employee can do some work at home

- discuss with the employee whether any special equipment is needed to help do the job safely, more easily or more effectively

- review whether any changes to the physical environment would be helpful

- consider whether it would be appropriate and reasonable to make exceptions to any of the employer's policies, procedures or practices, for example by exempting a disabled employee from the strict rules of an attendance procedure.

These are only examples, and the employer has a duty to take the initiative in order to establish what adjustments might be possible and practicable. Clearly any adjustment must be agreed with the individual employee, who will be the best judge of what, if anything, is required. Many workplace adjustments will cost little or nothing to implement and could help the employer to retain and motivate a valued member of staff.

In *Mid Staffordshire General Hospitals NHS Trust v Cambridge [2003] IRLR 566*, the EAT ruled that an employer should, in order to fulfil the duty to make reasonable adjustments, make an assessment of the employee's condition and prognosis, the effects of the condition on that person's ability to perform the relevant duties, the effect of the physical features of the workplace on the employee's ability to do the job and the steps that the employer could potentially take to reduce or remove the disadvantages that he or she is experiencing. The EAT stated further that the making of a proper assessment was a necessary precondition for fulfilment of the duty to make reasonable adjustments.

Managing an employee who has AIDS

One sensitive issue that needs to be carefully managed is the protection and support of an employee who has AIDS or who is HIV positive. The starting point is to view AIDS and HIV in the same light as any other illness, and treat absence from work on account of AIDS or HIV in exactly the same way as any other ill-health absence. However prejudice and ignorance about AIDS may lead to workplace problems such as an over-reaction on the part of colleagues if they learn of the employee's condition, potential harassment, or even an unwillingness of colleagues to work alongside the affected person. These issues need sensitive, but firm management.

Protection for employees with HIV or AIDS under the Disability Discrimination Act 1995

An employee who has AIDS will be expressly protected as a disabled person under the Disability Discrimination Act 1995 as soon as any symptoms develop. Someone who has been diagnosed as HIV positive, on the other hand, will not be regarded as disabled in law unless this causes symptoms that substantially affect his or her ability to carry out normal day-to-day activities. At the time of writing, however, a confirmed proposal is in the pipeline that, when implemented, will tighten up the provisions of the Act so that all workers who are diagnosed with HIV will fall under the scope of the Act from the point of diagnosis.

The earlier section titled 'Implications under the Disability Discrimination Act 1995' provides more information on the employer's duties under the Act.

Supporting an employee who has HIV or AIDS

In order to ensure that employees who have AIDS or HIV are fully protected and supported in their employment, employers should:

- devise and implement a policy on AIDS, the underlying aims of which should be to provide support to any employee who contracts the illness and prevent discrimination against him or her

- ensure the policy states clearly that the employer will not discriminate against any employee or job applicant who has HIV or AIDS

- provide information (perhaps in the form of written guidelines prepared by an occupational doctor) about HIV and AIDS, in order to educate employees about the infection and the fact that it cannot be spread through normal personal contact

- if it comes to light that an employee is HIV positive or has AIDS, seek confidential medical advice, especially if the employee's condition is likely to affect his or her ability to do the job, or if there might be safety implications

- recognise that with modern medication, employees with HIV will usually be able to continue to work normally and may not become ill for many years, if at all

- encourage an employee with AIDS to work as long as he or she is medically fit to do so, and if this person eventually becomes unfit to perform normal duties, give full consideration to redeployment or part-time working

- recognise that an employee with HIV or AIDS will be particularly vulnerable to harassment and take steps to prevent such harassment (see Chapter 4).

Offering time off and/or counselling

Employees who disclose that they have AIDS or HIV should be supported in the same way as an employee with any other long-term illness would be. If there are short-term absences from work, these should be treated in the same way as those of other employees on account of other illnesses. Statutory and occupational sick pay should be paid in line with normal procedures, and if the payment of occupational sick pay is discretionary, discretion should be exercised in the employee's favour. Generally, the type of support that should be offered would involve:

- offering to arrange counselling, if the employee wishes it

- allowing paid time off work for medical appointments and/or for counselling

- adopting a supportive attitude towards such employees and ensuring they know that the employer is on their side.

The issue of confidentiality

Once it comes to light that an employee has AIDS or is HIV positive (for example if the employee discloses the condition to a company doctor or to a senior manager), the employee should be asked whether he or she wishes to keep the matter confidential or would prefer to disclose it to colleagues, and if so how he or she would prefer the matter to be disclosed. If the employee expresses a preference for complete confidentiality, that should be respected, unless the employee's condition could pose a danger to others. Provided any first aiders in the organisation have been properly trained to use protective equipment, there should be no risk to their health and safety in the event that an employee with HIV infection requires first aid treatment. It follows that there would be no need for first aiders to be informed of someone's HIV status.

A policy on AIDS/HIV should state clearly that if an employee learns or suspects that a colleague is HIV infected or has AIDS, that employee must treat the information as strictly confidential, and that any breach of confidentiality in this matter will be regarded as a serious disciplinary offence that may result in summary dismissal. The only exception to this rule would be if the affected person worked in a job in which HIV infection could pose a risk to him/herself or to others.

Information about an individual's health is classed as 'sensitive data' under the Data Protection Act 1998, and as such cannot be recorded, used or disclosed without the person's express consent. Chapter 8 deals with data protection issues in relation to health records.

Dealing with instances of colleagues objecting to working alongside someone thought to have HIV or AIDS

Employers who have taken steps to educate and inform their workforce about HIV and AIDS will have reduced the likelihood of negative reactions occurring if it should come to light that someone in the workplace has the infection. Nevertheless if it is disclosed or suspected that an individual is HIV positive or has AIDS, there is the possibility that one or more employees may exhibit prejudice or react negatively. This may manifest itself in a refusal to work alongside the employee who is known or suspected to have the illness. In these circumstances quick and decisive action will be required from line management to deal with the problem and prevent it escalating. The manager should:

- consult with a member of occupational health staff to seek advice on the best way forward

- consult with HR staff to seek advice and guidance on how to handle the situation

- arrange to meet with the employees who are refusing to work alongside the person with HIV or AIDS

- provide information and reassurance about the nature of HIV and AIDS, and that these represent no threat to the health and safety of the person's colleagues (it may be helpful if an occupational doctor attends the meeting to answer any questions the staff may have)

- devise the discussions so that they are general in nature and not specific to the individual who is known or suspected to be infected

- inform employees that there is no reason, and no justification, for any refusal to work alongside a person who is HIV positive or who has AIDS, and that any lack of cooperation will not be tolerated by the employer

- advise employees that people who have AIDS are protected by the Disability Discrimination Act and that the employer is obliged under that Act to ensure there is no discrimination and also to support such an employee by making reasonable adjustments

- instruct employees that any harassment, victimisation or detrimental treatment of an employee on account of his or her HIV or AIDS status would be discriminatory in law, that such conduct will not be tolerated and that it will be regarded as gross misconduct, potentially leading to summary dismissal

- monitor the situation to ensure that the employee is not experiencing any further difficulties.

Managing an employee who is mentally ill

A report titled *Out at Work*, published by the Mental Health Foundation in 2002, suggested that three out of every 10 employees would be likely to experience mental health problems in the course of any one year. Furthermore, the CBI has estimated that a third of all sickness absence is due to mental health issues. Unlike most types of physical ill health, mental ill health often carries with it a stigma, causing fear in others and a tendency, through ignorance, to shun those with such illness, rather than supporting them.

The Health Education Authority in 1997 defined mental health as: 'the emotional and spiritual resilience which allows us to enjoy life and to survive pain, disappointment and sadness. It is a positive sense of wellbeing and an underlying belief in our own and others' dignity and worth.' This broad definition indicates that the protection and promotion of employees' mental health is at least as important as the promotion of their physical health and safety, if not more so.

Many factors will influence an employee's mental health. Personal factors, including family and financial matters, social networks, feelings of belonging and participating, self-esteem and the ability to cope with day-to-day issues and exercise control over work and home life will all play their part, among many others. It follows that employers can have a great deal of influence on an employee's mental wellbeing and can promote mental health by paying attention to such factors as:

- meaningful communication and involvement for all staff at all levels in the organisation

- constructive feedback and praise, so that employees feel valued

- reassurance in times of change

- encouragement for employees to come forward in the event that they have any worries, concerns or anxieties in the workplace

- an effective grievance procedure in which it is made clear that no employee will be penalised in any way for raising a genuine concern or complaint about workplace matters

- opportunities to develop skills and gain opportunities for career progression

- giving employees influence and control over their work and the way it is done wherever possible

- work–life balance

- effective measures to prevent and deal with workplace stress

- effective measures to prevent and deal with bullying and harassment in the workplace

- developing a positive workplace culture.

Even where the employer has taken positive steps to promote employees' mental wellbeing, an employee may nevertheless experience mental ill health, which may, in turn, cause the employer difficulties. The nature of mental illness will be sensitive and its course may be unpredictable. Nevertheless, an employee who has a mental illness should essentially be supported as much as someone with a physical illness, with possibly an even greater degree of tolerance and support being shown. Advice should be sought from an occupational doctor, who should be asked to recommend the most appropriate and supportive courses of action.

Mental ill health may take many forms, ranging from serious long-term illnesses such as schizophrenia through to common conditions such as depression, ME (each of which may itself range from mild to severe) and some stress-related illnesses.

Employees with clinically well-recognised mental illnesses are protected under the Disability Discrimination Act 1995, which provides that treating an employee unfavourably on the grounds of a disability amounts to unlawful discrimination. At the time of writing, a draft Bill proposes to remove the provision that requires a mental illness to be clinically recognised before the person can claim protection under the Act. This change, when implemented (expected in late 2005), will mean that many people with many stress-related illnesses will fall within the scope of the Act even if their condition does not have a formal psychiatric diagnosis. Provided the condition has a substantial and long-term adverse effect on their ability to carry out normal day-to-day activities, they will be protected.

The Disability Discrimination Act also imposes on employers the duty to make reasonable adjustments to working practices. Such reasonable adjustments could, in the case of an employee with a mental illness or mental impairment, include:

- allowing an employee with a mental illness more time off work or more frequent periods of short-term absence than would normally be acceptable

- providing longer or more frequent rest breaks and, if possible, a quiet place for an employee to escape to for a break in times of pressure

- consulting the employee to establish whether a reduction in working hours would be helpful

- allowing a later or flexible start-time, as many employees with mental illness may have difficulty with sleeping patterns and stamina due either to the symptoms of their illness or to medication prescribed to control it

- adjusting the employee's job duties (possibly temporarily), for example exempting the employee from any aspect of the job that is particularly stressful (if the illness is stress-related), removing him or her from frontline duties or reducing the workload

- being flexible as to methods of working and pace of working (within overall parameters)

- exhibiting tolerance and sympathy to erratic behaviour at work (up to a reasonable degree)

- providing additional supervision, coaching or mentoring, for example for an employee who has learning difficulties

- providing access to counselling with someone who has mental health expertise

- arranging for someone to act as buddy or mentor for the employee with a view to providing day-to-day support

- allowing the employee to work partly at home, if this would be helpful.

In *London Borough of Hillingdon v Morgan EAT 1493/98*, an office-based employee had been off work with ME for approximately eight months. When she began to recover, her GP had recommended that she should be allowed to work part time from home for a temporary period to help her to ease back into full-time employment. The employer, however, refused to contemplate such an arrangement. When she claimed that this amounted to an unlawful failure to make reasonable adjustments under the Disability Discrimination Act, the EAT agreed and stated that there was no proper reason why the employee's request could not have been accommodated.

Ultimately, if the employer promotes a positive working environment and provides appropriate support at work, this will help to:

- reduce the likelihood of absence on account of stress-related illness

- facilitate the rehabilitation of an employee who has had an absence from work on account of mental ill health

- improve the long-term outlook for any employee who does experience mental health problems.

The last resort: dismissal

Where an employee has been off sick for a lengthy period of time and there is no prospect of a recovery and return to work in the foreseeable future, the employer may ultimately have to consider terminating that person's contract on the grounds of incapacity.

Whether and when dismissal is an option

An employer should only consider dismissal when:

- the employee's continuing absence is causing operational difficulties for the employer

- medical advice is that the employee is unlikely to be fit to resume work in the foreseeable future

- the employer has made all possible reasonable adjustments to support the employee's rehabilitation

- all other options in relation to the employee's continuing employment have been exhausted

- there is no early retirement provision available to the employee that he or she finds acceptable.

If the illness amounts to a disability in law, the employers will also need to ensure that, before taking a decision to dismiss, they have addressed their minds to what reasonable adjustments could be made to facilitate the employee's return to work. In *Fu v London Borough of Camden [2001] IRLR 186*, the EAT stated that an employer was under a duty to do everything reasonably possible to retain a disabled person in employment.

How to follow fair procedures when dismissing an employee on grounds of long-term ill health

All employers should devise and implement clear and transparent procedures for termination of employment in a range of circumstances, including incapacity on the grounds of ill health.

General principles applicable to the fairness of a dismissal on the grounds of long-term ill health

Under section 98 of the Employment Rights Act 1996, dismissal on the grounds of lack of 'capability' can be fair. 'Capability' is defined as being 'assessed by reference to skill, aptitude, health or any other physical or mental quality'. The Act also requires employers to act reasonably in all the circumstances in treating the reason for dismissal as sufficient to justify dismissal.

These legal principles are well established in law. In addition, courts and tribunals have judged that the fairness or otherwise of a dismissal on grounds of long-term ill health will depend on a range of factors, namely:

- the size and resources of the employer's business

- the level of seniority and degree of specialisation of the employee's job

- the degree of disruption that the employee's absence is creating for the business

- the effect of the employee's absence on colleagues

- the urgency and importance of having the employee's work done

- the feasibility or otherwise of employing a temporary replacement to cover the employee's work

- the length of the employee's absence(s) to date

- the nature and pattern of any previous absences

- the likelihood of the employee being able to return to work in the near future.

There is no legal time limit after which dismissal will be considered to be fair; instead each case stands to be judged on its own merits. Ultimately if, in all the circumstances of the case, the employer cannot reasonably be expected in view of its business requirements to wait any longer for the employee to recover and return to work, dismissal may be fair at that point.

Statutory dismissal procedure

New measures introduced in October 2004 under the Employment Act 2002 (Dispute Resolution) Regulations 2004 oblige all organisations (including small employers) to follow a statutory dismissal and disciplinary procedure (DDP) before deciding to dismiss an employee. The basic statutory procedure involves a three-stage process, obliging the employer to:

- set out the employee's circumstances' in writing and give or send a copy to the employee, inviting him or her to attend a meeting to discuss the matter

- hold a meeting to discuss the situation and enable both parties to explain their cases prior to any decision being taken (the employee will have the right to be accompanied at this meeting by a colleague or trade union representative)

- allow a right of appeal against any decision to dismiss, which should be to a more senior person.

The regulations state that an employee must take all reasonable steps to attend the meeting. However, if this is not practicable due to illness, then technically the procedure will not apply. The employer is, however, under a duty to ensure that the timing and location of any meeting is reasonable. To fulfil that duty, it may be necessary, for example, to arrange for the meeting to take place in the employee's home (subject to the employee finding such an arrangement acceptable).

Ensuring fairness in procedure

Where someone is absent from work due to genuine illness, it is obvious that application of the employer's disciplinary procedure would be inappropriate. Such an approach might upset the employee and even, in certain circumstances, lead to an exacerbation of the illness. Instead, the employer should adopt a 'capability procedure'. To ensure fairness and reasonableness, the employer's capability procedure should include the following steps:

- review the employee's sickness/absence record thoroughly

- obtain up-to-date medical advice regarding the likelihood of the employee being able to return to work and, if that may be feasible, whether he or she would be capable of full or only partial job performance

- write to the employee informing them that the employer wishes to review the circumstances of the ongoing absence and to arrange a meeting

- ensure the timing and location of the meeting is suitable for the employee

- inform the employee that he or she has the right to be accompanied at the meeting by a colleague or trade union representative

- at the meeting, discuss the employee's absence, its effects on the business and the courses of action open to the employer, including the fact that termination is now being seriously considered

- listen to any representations that the employee may wish to make and take full account of his or her opinions and feelings regarding the illness and ongoing absence from work

- if appropriate, review in conjunction with the employee the possibility of resuming work on a part-time basis, or with different or lighter duties

- after the meeting, make a decision on whether to terminate, taking all relevant factors into account

- communicate the outcome of the meeting to the employee in writing

- allow a right of appeal if the decision is taken to dismiss the employee.

The general principles required for fairness were nicely summed up by the EAT in the case of *East Lindsey District Council v Daubney [1977] IRLR 181*. The EAT stated:

> Unless there are wholly exceptional circumstances, before an employee is dismissed on the grounds of ill health, it is necessary that he should be consulted and the matter discussed with him, and that in one way or another steps should be taken by the employer to discover the true medical position. ... Only one thing is certain, and that is that if the employee is not consulted, and given an opportunity to state his case, an injustice may be done.

Equally, if an employee is dismissed for incapacity without the input of professional medical advice, an employment tribunal would be likely to take the view that the employer had acted unreasonably in not taking available medical evidence into account before taking the decision to dismiss the employee. This would render the dismissal unfair in law.

The importance of checking the employee's statutory and contractual rights

Before a decision is taken to dismiss an employee on the grounds of continuing ill-health absence, the employee's statutory and contractual rights should be reviewed.

Statutory entitlement to notice

A little known provision in the Employment Rights Act 1996 ss88–89 entitles an employee whose employment is terminated and who is unable to work during the notice period as a result of illness to be paid at the normal level of pay during the statutory notice period. Statutory notice is equivalent to one week's notice for each completed year of service up to a maximum of 12 weeks. Thus, if the employee is no longer receiving any occupational sick pay, his or her normal pay would have to be reactivated for the duration of their statutory notice period.

Strangely, these provisions do not come into operation if the employee's contract contains a notice period that is more than one week longer than the statutory notice to which they would be entitled. This can have the peculiar result that an employee whose contractual notice period happens to be the same as his or her statutory entitlement will benefit from the right to paid notice, while another employee whose contract stipulates a longer period of contractual notice will not have the right to the benefit of paid notice. In the event that an employee does not benefit from this statutory provision, entitlement to pay during the notice period will stand to be determined according to the terms of the employee's contract.

Contractual rights to sickness benefit

Another important point that the employer should review before making a decision to dismiss is whether termination of the employee's employment might be in breach of contract by depriving them of entitlement to long-term sickness benefits to which he or she has a contractual right. In particular, if the employer has a permanent health insurance scheme in place, it is probable that the terms of the scheme are such that benefit will be payable only to current employees who are incapacitated, and not to those whose contracts have been terminated for any reason. If this is the case, then it would be a breach of contract to dismiss an employee on account of long-term sickness absence, because to do so would take away a benefit to which that person was entitled under their contract.

POINTS TO NOTE

- The underlying objective of long-term ill-health management will be to achieve an acceptable and fair balance between the protection and promotion of employee health and wellbeing on the one hand and the needs of the business on the other.

- The starting point for the effective management of long-term ill-health absence is the creation of effective policies and procedures.

- A policy on ill-health absence should (among other things) indicate an overall supportive approach towards employees who experience long-term sickness, explain what benefits employees will be entitled to receive, state the role of occupational health, clarify how contact will be maintained during periods of absence and outline what measures will be adopted to facilitate rehabilitation.

- It is very important to carefully manage an employee's return to work after a lengthy period of sickness absence and to give due consideration to the employee's concerns.

- An employee whose illness has lasted, or is likely to last, 12 months or more and has a substantial adverse effect on their ability to carry out normal day-to-day activities will be protected against discriminatory treatment by the Disability Discrimination Act.

- All employers are obliged under the Disability Discrimination Act to make 'reasonable adjustments' to their working practices to accommodate the needs of a disabled employee.

- An employee who has AIDS is expressly protected as a disabled person under the Disability Discrimination Act 1995.

- Employees who disclose that they have AIDS or HIV should be supported in the same way as staff with any other long-term illness would be supported.

- Employers can promote employees' mental health by paying attention to factors such as open communication, effective feedback, and the establishment of policies on stress, bullying, effective grievance handling and work–life balance.

- If the employer promotes a positive working environment and provides appropriate support at work, this is likely to reduce significantly the level of absence caused by stress-related illness.

- An employer should only consider dismissing an employee who is absent from work long term once all other options in relation to the employee's continuing employment have been exhausted.

- Although dismissal on the grounds of incapacity can be fair, employment law requires employers to act reasonably in all the circumstances.

ACTION POINTS

- Maintain regular contact with any employees who are absent from work due to long-term sickness.

- State clearly in employees' written terms of employment what, if any, occupational sick pay will be paid to employees who are unable to attend work due to sickness, and any conditions for eligibility for payment.

- Consult all relevant staff about how an absent employee's work is to be covered, rather than leaving the matter to chance.

- Ensure that, in arranging for the absent employee's work to be covered, no colleagues are overloaded or required to take on duties that they are not fully trained to do, or capable of doing.

- Arrange for an employee who is ready to return to work after a period of long-term sickness absence to be examined by an occupational doctor to check that the employee is genuinely fit to work and establish whether he or she should be exempted initially from any particular job duties.

- Take positive steps to help an employee who has been absent for a long time to reintegrate into the workplace, having first consulted the employee about any proposed measures.

- Monitor the situation over the first few weeks after an employee's return to work in order to ensure he or she is coping with the workload and the day-to-day pressures inherent in the workplace.

- Consult an employee whose illness amounts to a disability in law as to what workplace adjustments might be helpful to the employee and reasonable for the employer to implement.

- Allow an employee who has returned to work following long-term illness to take reasonable time off work with pay to attend medical appointments or therapy (if the employee requires such time off).

- Allow an employee who has been seriously ill flexibility in the number of hours he or she works for a period of time after his or her return.

- Recognise that prejudice and ignorance about AIDS may lead to problems such as harassment or refusal to work alongside the employee, and that such problems will need sensitive but firm management.

- Provide information about HIV and AIDS to all employees in order to educate them about the infection and the fact that it cannot be spread through normal personal contact.

- Encourage any employees with AIDS to work as long as they are medically fit to do so, and if they eventually become unfit to perform their normal duties, give full consideration to redeployment or part-time working.

- Adopt a 'capability procedure' to deal with employees who experience long-term sickness absence, and ensure the procedure includes medical advice, consultation with the employees and consideration of whether they could be moved to alternative or part-time work.

- Review whether termination of an employee's employment might be in breach of contract by depriving that person of entitlement to long-term sickness benefits to which he or she has a contractual right.

CHAPTER 8

MEDICAL ADVICE AND HEALTH RECORDS

Introduction

In order to promote the effective management of employees' health and wellbeing, and deal competently and fairly with cases of long-term ill health, it will be necessary for employers in a variety of circumstances to be able to obtain medical advice about an employee.

This section aims to explore when and how employers should seek medical advice about their employees, taking into account human rights and data protection implications, as well as the provisions of the Access to Medical Reports Act 1988.

Circumstances in which the employer may wish to seek medical advice about an employee

There are various circumstances in which an employer may wish to obtain medical advice about a particular employee. Such circumstances could include the need to:

- ensure a job applicant is fit to perform the duties of the job for which he or she has applied

- obtain information about the state of health and likelihood of recovery of an employee who is absent from work due to sickness

- establish the likely length of time an employee will be absent from work, so that the employer can decide what arrangements to make to cover that person's work

- check that an employee who is ready to return to work after a long period of sickness absence is genuinely fit to resume working

- determine whether an employee who is unfit to perform his or her own job might be capable of performing a different one, for example lighter duties or part-time work

- assess what, if any, adjustments would be appropriate for an employee who has a disability in order to facilitate his or her continued employment

- review whether an employee who has frequently taken short periods off work has an underlying medical condition that is causing the absences

- assess the health of an employee to work at nights (as required by Regulation 7 of the Working Time Regulations)

- satisfy legal or other requirements with regard to an employee's prospective overseas posting

- assess whether an employee is well enough to attend a meeting, for example a disciplinary interview

- review the health and fitness of employees who work in hazardous conditions or whose jobs require a higher than usual standard of fitness

- screen employees for alcohol or drugs (see Chapter 5)

- assess an employee's eligibility for benefit under a long-term ill-health benefit scheme or for ill-health early retirement.

The employer may also wish to offer routine medical examinations on a voluntary basis as a perk of the job.

Assessing whether an employee is well enough to attend a meeting

Even though an employee has been signed off work by a doctor, that does not necessarily mean he or she is not well enough to communicate with the employer, take telephone calls, receive home visits or even attend a meeting at the workplace (or at some other mutually agreed venue such as a private room in a hotel near to the employee's home).

There may be a range of circumstances in which the employer might wish to hold a meeting with someone who is absent from work, for example to review the employee's job duties and general circumstances of employment, to progress an outstanding performance or disciplinary matter, to discuss what the employer could do to facilitate the worker's recovery and/or return to work, or to agree specific arrangements just before someone returns to work.

The most sensible course of action for an employer who is concerned that it might be unfair or discriminatory to require an employee to attend a meeting while signed off sick is to seek advice from an occupational doctor (if the employer has access to such a service), or alternatively (with the employee's consent) write to the employee's GP to ask whether the patient would be fit to attend the particular type of meeting the employer wishes to arrange.

The employer should of course explain clearly to the employee what the purpose of the meeting would be, what issues would be up for discussion, and the hoped-for outcomes. These points should be confirmed in writing. Depending on the type of meeting, the employee may have the right to be accompanied by a colleague or trade union official of his or her choice. This right will apply whenever the meeting is a disciplinary hearing that might result in action being taken against the employee, or a formal grievance hearing. The employee should, where appropriate, be advised in writing of the right to be accompanied.

The employer should exercise caution (but not necessarily back off altogether) if the employee alleges that the prospect of a meeting will cause stress or otherwise exacerbate an illness. Such a claim may of course be absolutely genuine, and if so should be respected. It is, however, not uncommon for an employee to 'play the stress card' in order to avoid facing disciplinary action or a meeting to discuss inadequate standards of performance. A doctor's view on whether the employee is well enough to attend the meeting should be sought and respected.

If the meeting cannot take place on medical grounds, the employee should be advised in writing that:

- The performance or disciplinary proceedings (as appropriate) have been suspended temporarily as a consequence of the employee's ill health.

- It will nevertheless be necessary to reactivate the proceedings in the future once the employee is well enough to attend a meeting to discuss the matter.

- It is likely to be in the employee's best interests to have the meeting sooner rather than later in order to conclude the matter and avoid allowing it to drag out over a long period of time.

In other words, the employer should make it clear that the performance or disciplinary matter has not been dropped and will still have to be dealt with one way or another in the future. This should be stated factually and without any hint of pressure. Ideally the letter should also include a statement that the employer is genuinely concerned to protect the employee's health and support him or her in any reasonable way, while at the same time adhering to fair procedures to ensure the employer's business interests are consistently maintained.

In these circumstances the employee should be provided with a written summary of the status of the proceedings: the case against him or her, what has occurred to date and what the next stage of the relevant procedure will be when it is reactivated.

Considering whether a home visit is appropriate

The employer should be flexible as regards the timing and location of any meeting with an employee who is off work due to sickness. Furthermore, reasonable notice should always be given (at least a few days).

It might be reasonable to suggest to the employee that the meeting could be held at home, but this would of course require the employee's consent and no undue pressure should be put on anyone to agree to such a course of action. If the person concerned lives some distance from the workplace and/or is not well enough to travel, an alternative might be to meet in a private room in a hotel located in the vicinity of his or her home. If this is agreed, the employer should undertake to make the appropriate arrangements and perhaps also arrange for a taxi to pick the employee up at home and take them to the hotel.

The relevance of obtaining medical advice in respect of an employee who has had frequent short-term absences

Where someone has had frequent short-term absences from work, there may be a single underlying cause or a variety of causes. The employer may even suspect that the employee is malingering, or taking time off work without good reason. Such a suspicion may, or may not, be well founded.

It may, however, be helpful for an employer in these circumstances to obtain medical advice in order to ascertain or confirm whether any underlying medical condition is causing the employee's frequent absences. A medical report may reveal that the employee has a condition that flares up from time to time, thus providing evidence that absences are genuine. Conversely, the report may conclude that the employee is fit and healthy in a general sense. Even in this case, however, the employer should not immediately jump to negative conclusions, as it may be that this person is simply more prone than most to affliction with common ailments such as flu or colds. Nevertheless, the opportunity for the employee to be medically examined and for a report to be provided to the employer will provide both parties with a sound and fair basis for discussion if the absences start to become excessive and/or cause operational problems for the employer.

Human rights and data protection implications

Before requiring an employee to undergo a medical examination, the employer should have a clear aim in mind. Any requirement for someone to undergo a medical examination, or any application to his or her GP for a medical report, will represent an intrusion into that person's privacy under Article 8 of the Human Rights Act 1998 (the right to respect for private and family life, home and correspondence).

The Human Rights Act 1998 essentially gives individuals a range of rights in relation to their treatment by public authorities. Thus, employees of public authorities would be able to take a direct claim against their employer to a court or tribunal if they had grounds to believe that the employer had breached their right to privacy. Although the Act does not confer any similar benefit on private sector employees, there is a separate provision in the Act that obliges courts and tribunals (as public authorities themselves) to interpret legislation in such a way as is compatible with the rights contained in the European Convention on Human Rights, and by extension the Human Rights Act 1998. Thus private sector workers benefit too, albeit indirectly.

One of the key principles underpinning the Human Rights Act is the principle of proportionality. This essentially means that there should be a balance between the rights of individuals under the Act and the general interests of the community at large. The right of individuals to respect for their privacy is therefore not an absolute right, but stands to be balanced proportionally against the rights and freedoms of others. 'Others' in this context includes employers.

Thus, where an employer operates a policy of requiring staff to undergo medical examinations with occupational doctors, the principle of proportionality may well permit this even though medical examinations represent an invasion of privacy. The policy will be justified if it is proportionate to the achievement of a legitimate aim. This means that the employer would have to be able to demonstrate that the policy was designed to achieve a legitimate business aim (for example to facilitate workplace adjustments for a disabled employee) and the type of medical examination required was proportionate to that aim, that is to say, not excessive in relation to the aim to be achieved.

Medical screening should not therefore be conducted arbitrarily, but rather should be carried out with a specific, justifiable purpose in mind. Furthermore, screening should not be any more rigorous than is required for the attainment of the specified purpose; for example the employer should not require a standard of fitness that is higher than is necessary for the effective performance of a particular job.

Over and above the requirements of the Human Rights Act 1998, employers need to comply with the Data Protection Act 1998 whenever the results of a medical examination are recorded in any form (which of course is inevitable). Part 4 of the Employment Practices Data Protection Code (which covers workers' health) recommends that employers should conduct medical examinations on existing employees only where they are satisfied that testing is a necessary and justified means of:

- ensuring health and safety in the workplace

- determining employees' fitness for continued employment

- establishing entitlement to health related benefits, for example payment of occupational sick pay or eligibility to join a pension or insurance scheme

- preventing discrimination against an employee who has a disability.

Using occupational doctors

Many employers use the services of an occupational doctor. Larger employers may employ a doctor and/or nurse on a full-time basis while employers whose size and resources do not justify such appointments may prefer to contract with a local firm of occupational health specialists to provide certain defined services, whether on a regular or ad hoc basis.

An occupational doctor, in particular a doctor who works for the employer or who has experience of the employer's industry sector, will be likely to have a sound understanding of the particular employee's working conditions, the demands that the job places upon people, any special hazards or demands inherent in the workplace and any specific issues associated with rehabilitation into the workplace. Conversely, an occupational doctor is unlikely to have full knowledge of a particular employee's medical history or general background without reference to that person's GP.

Whether occupational health is in-house or on contract to an external firm, if the employer wishes to make the most effective use of the service, it will be necessary to include a clause in every employee's contract to the effect that staff must consent to attend a medical examination with an occupational doctor nominated by the employer whenever asked to do so (for any reason). The contract should also specify that the employee will consent to the occupational doctor providing a confidential report to the employer following any such examination.

If such contractual clauses are not in place, employers could be in breach of contract if they put pressure on an employee to agree to a doctor's examination. Such conduct may also constitute a breach of the right to privacy under Article 8 of the Human Rights Act 1998 (see above under 'Human rights and data protection implications'). This could give rise to a claim for constructive dismissal (subject to the employee having a minimum of one year's service) if someone chose to resign on account of the employer's behaviour.

Despite this concern, it is of course open to an employer who has not had the foresight to include such clauses in a contract simply to request consent at the time medical evidence is being sought. Some employees may be quite at ease with such a request and may even welcome the opportunity to be examined by an independent doctor who can provide an objective opinion on their condition or general state of health and fitness.

A model contractual clause could be in the terms shown in the 'Model contract clause' box.

> ## Model contract clause
>
> It is a condition of your contract of employment that you agree, when asked to do so by the Company for any reason, to undergo a medical examination(s) by an occupational doctor nominated by the Company. The Company will explain to you the reason(s) for any such request, and meet all costs associated with the examination. You agree also to authorise the doctor(s) who conduct the medical examination(s) to prepare a medical report detailing the results of the examination(s) for disclosure to and discussion with the Company.
>
> A refusal without good reason to consent to attend a medical examination with an occupational doctor when asked to do so by the Company will be regarded as a breach of contract leading potentially to disciplinary proceedings against you.

It will be to the employer's considerable advantage to ensure that every employee's contract contains such a clause. A contractual requirement to agree to be medically examined would also have the effect that anyone who refused to attend a medical examination with an occupational doctor when asked to do so would be acting in breach of contract. This would allow the employer to take appropriate disciplinary action against the employee, provided the request itself was reasonable and the refusal was without good reason. It would also be important to incorporate clear statements in the employer's sickness absence policy and disciplinary procedure to the effect that a breach of the rules in this respect would be regarded as a disciplinary offence.

The Access to Medical Reports Act 1988 will not normally apply to medical reports prepared by an independent occupational doctor, unless the doctor in question also happens to be the employee's GP or specialist. Consequently, it is usually easier for employers to obtain medical advice about their employees from an occupational doctor than from GPs (see also below under 'Key provisions of the Access to Medical Reports Act 1988') because they will not need to seek the employee's express consent each time a report is prepared.

Seeking medical reports from an employee's GP

Where an employer needs to obtain medical advice about an employee, it may be desirable to seek information from more than one source. This approach would be particularly recommended if dismissal or ill-health retirement was being contemplated. Thus, the employer may, in addition to arranging for an examination by an occupational doctor, wish to seek information from the employee's GP and/or possibly from the employee's specialist or private consultant if this is appropriate. Often the organisation's occupational doctor will be the person with responsibility for putting things in motion to obtain medical advice from the GP.

The employer should always provide sufficient meaningful information to the doctor from whom a medical report is sought, and also ask specific relevant questions, so that the doctor can make a reasoned judgment on the employee's fitness to work.

Relevant information to provide to the doctor will include:

- the reason the examination or report is required, for example to review whether an employee who has frequently taken short periods off has an underlying medical condition that might be causing these absences

- some background regarding the employee's job and working environment

- any specific features of the job that may create special risks, for example if the job involves regular overtime working or night-shift working, if the job is particularly stressful or if the employee is likely to come into contact with hazardous substances in the course of doing the work

- any relevant background on the person's employment record, for example high rates of absenteeism or complaints about workplace stress.

Specific questions that the employer may wish to consider asking the doctor could include:

- the likely timescale within which the employee may recover and be fit to resume working

- whether the employee is likely to recover fully or to remain partly incapacitated in some way in the longer term

- whether the condition is likely to recur after the employee has returned to work

- whether an employee who is unfit to perform his or her normal job may be well enough to do lighter duties or part-time work

- whether the employee is fit to perform specific duties (which should be explained), such as heavy physical work or work that is known to be particularly stressful.

Key provisions of the Access to Medical Reports Act 1988

In order to be able to obtain a medical report from an employee's GP, specialist or private consultant, the employer will need to abide by the provisions of the Access to Medical Reports Act 1988.

The Access to Medical Reports Act gives individuals a variety of rights in relation to 'any medical report relating to the individual which is to be, or has been, supplied by a medical practitioner for employment purposes'. It also imposes limitations on employers as regards the extent to which they may seek and obtain information from an individual's own doctor.

The Act further states that it applies to medical reports that are 'prepared by a medical practitioner who is or has been responsible for the clinical care of the individual'. This means that the provisions of the Act are limited to medical reports prepared by an employee's own doctor, specialist or consultant. Reports prepared by occupational doctors will not be subject to the Act unless the doctor in question also happens to be responsible for the clinical care of the individual concerned.

Employees have the following rights under the Act:

- to be informed by their employer in writing if the employer wishes to contact their GP for a medical report

- to refuse to allow the employer to apply to their GP for a medical report

- to be given a copy of the report by the doctor once it has been prepared (within 21 days)

- to ask the doctor to amend the report, if they consider it to be inaccurate or misleading

- to refuse to allow the report to be released to the employer.

Employers wishing to seek a medical report from an employee's GP must therefore start the process by informing the employee in writing of their intention, and requesting written consent to this course of action. The letter must also inform the employee of his or her rights under the Act. These steps must be taken before the employer contacts the GP.

The employee has the statutory right to refuse to give consent and the employer must respect this decision. In this context, it is worth noting that any term in an employee's contract that purports to require the employee to agree to the provision of a GP's report will be void, because such a term would contradict the rights afforded to employees under statutory law.

If the employee who does give consent expresses a wish to have access to the doctor's report before it is sent to the employer, the employer must inform the doctor in writing of this fact when applying for the report, and at the same time inform the employee in writing that the application has been made.

Even when an employee agrees to allow the employer to contact the doctor for a report, that is not the end of the matter. Once the report has been prepared, the employee has the right of access to it, and may at that stage refuse to allow it to be disclosed to the employer. Again, the employee has the absolute right under the Act to make this decision.

Dealing with employees who refuse to cooperate with their employer

If there is no clause in employees' contracts obliging them to agree to be examined by an occupational doctor at the employer's request, the employer will be reliant on their willingness to agree at the time to undergo a medical examination with an occupational doctor.

Furthermore, as explained above under 'Key provisions of the Access to Medical Reports Act 1988', employees have the absolute right to refuse to give their consent for the employer to apply for a medical report from their own GP.

It may transpire, therefore, that the employer is prevented from obtaining medical evidence about a particular employee because that person will neither consent to undergo a medical examination with an occupational doctor nor authorise the employer to apply to the GP for a medical report. The possible implications of this scenario are that:

- the employer may consider that the employee's lack of cooperation is unreasonable and even that it represents a breach of the implied duty to cooperate, which is inherent in every contract of employment

- if decisions have to made about that person's ongoing employment and/or rehabilitation, the employer will have no option but to base any decision on whatever facts are available at the time.

In these circumstances, the employer should meet with the employee and explain the possible consequences of a refusal to cooperate. If a meeting is not possible, then the circumstances should be explained in writing. It may be that the employee can be persuaded to cooperate, although no unfair pressure should be put on him or her to do so. The employee should also be clearly and fairly informed of any possible consequences of a refusal to cooperate, without of course any undertone of threat or disapproval. In particular, if dismissal on grounds of long-term ill-health absence has become a serious option, the employee should be informed of this fact.

Similarly if the employer wishes to establish whether or not a particular workplace adjustment would be appropriate to ease an employee's rehabilitation into the workplace, it should be explained that the absence of medical advice makes it very difficult for the employer to make a reasoned decision. The employer should explain in a sympathetic way that any decisions that have to be made about future employment will be for the better if the employee agrees to permit a medical examination and/or medical report.

Key provisions of the Data Protection Act 1998 relevant to health records

Whenever an employer collects or holds any information about employees' health or sickness absence, the provisions of the Data Protection Act 1998 will apply.

The Act applies to any organisation that collects, holds or in any way uses data (i.e. information) about people, where individuals can be identified from the data. Thus, whenever employers record information about their staff, they will be obliged to adhere to the requirements of the Act. All recorded information is covered, including data held in paper format, on computer or on microfiche, and information contained in the body of e-mail correspondence. Collecting, retaining and using information about individuals (known as 'personal data') is referred to as 'data processing'.

Key aims of the Data Protection Act

The key aims of the Data Protection Act 1998 in the context of employment are to:

- strike a reasonable balance between the needs of employers to hold records about their employees for specific purposes and the rights of those employees to respect for their private life

- protect the rights of individuals with regard to information held about them by their employer, in particular their right to privacy

- require employers to comply with eight data protection principles which are set out in the Act (see below under 'The data protection principles')

- regulate what employers may, or may not, do with personal information once they have collected it

- allow employees to gain access to any information held about them (on request).

Certain information relating to individuals is regarded as 'sensitive data' under the Act, and such information is subject to special provisions and restrictions that do not apply to the collection of ordinary information. Data about employees' physical and mental health falls into the category of sensitive data (see below under 'When health information constitutes sensitive data under the Data Protection Act').

Employees' rights under the Data Protection Act

Employees and other workers have a range of rights under the Data Protection Act. The rights are for all individuals to:

- be informed if the employer is processing personal data about them

- be given a description of the data

- be informed of the purpose(s) for which the data is held

- be told to whom the data may be disclosed and for what purpose(s) it may be disclosed

- have any inaccuracies in the data corrected or removed on request

- seek compensation if they have suffered any damage or distress as a result of the employer breaching the Data Protection Act

- be given a copy of the data held about them on written request (and on payment of a fee of up to £10, if the employer so requires).

The data protection principles

There are eight data protection principles contained in Schedule 1 of the Data Protection Act 1998, with which all organisations that hold personal data about individuals must comply. These state that employers must:

1. Process personal data fairly and lawfully (which essentially means that the employee must have given consent to processing, or that the data must be necessary for reasons related to legal obligations, justice, contract or other legitimate business interests).

2. Obtain personal data only for specified and lawful purposes, and not process the data for any purpose(s) that is incompatible with the stated purposes.

3. Ensure all data held is adequate, relevant and not excessive in relation to the purpose(s) for which it was obtained.

4. Ensure data is accurate and, where necessary, kept up to date.

5. Not keep data for longer than is necessary in relation to the purpose(s) for which it was obtained (although no specific time periods are prescribed in the Act).

6. Process data in accordance with individuals' rights under the Act.

7. Take appropriate measures to protect data against unauthorised or unlawful processing, accidental loss or destruction, and damage.

8. Not transfer personal data outside the European Economic Area unless the country to which it is transferred has an adequate level of protection in place for individuals' rights and freedoms in relation to the processing of personal data.

Judging whether it is justifiable to hold health data about employees

The Data Protection Act 1998 does not prevent employers from collecting or using health information about their employees. Nevertheless, the ways in which an employer may use health data about individuals is restricted and the collection and use of such information must be justified by one of a list of sensitive-data conditions (see below under 'Conditions for the processing of health information').

Employers should always review objectively the question of whether the collection and use of health data about their employees is necessary, and the specific purpose or purposes for which the data is necessary.

The Employment Practices Data Protection Code

The Employment Practices Data Protection Code consists of four separate parts, dealing with:

- recruitment and selection (Part 1)

- employment records (Part 2)

- monitoring at work (Part 3)

- information about workers' health (Part 4).

Part 4 of the Code (workers' health) covers a range of issues, including occupational health data, medical testing, drug screening and genetic testing.

The Code, like other codes of practice, does not impose legally binding duties on employers. Nevertheless, if it comes to light at a court or tribunal that an employer has failed to follow its key recommendations, this would act to the employer's detriment. This is because it provides for collection of material that can be used in evidence, and non-compliance could therefore be used to strengthen an employee's claim against the employer. It is therefore in every employer's interests to comply with the recommendations contained in the Code, which in any event is a useful source of practical guidance. Essentially, the Code represents the Information Commissioner's interpretation of the steps employers need to take to ensure compliance with the Data Protection Act, and it follows that compliance with the Code should ensure compliance with the Act.

Key provisions of Part 4 of the Code on health records

Some of the key provisions of part 4 of the Employment Practices Data Protection Code are that employers should:

- conduct an impact assessment to establish whether there is justification for collecting and holding different types of health information about employees (see below under 'Carrying out an impact assessment')

- leave the assessment of health issues, including judgements about an employee's fitness to work to qualified medical practitioners

- only allow HR professionals and line managers to have access to details about an employee's health or medical condition where they need to have access to such information, and otherwise restrict their access to information about whether or not the employee is fit to perform his or her job duties and/or whether there are legitimate reasons for absences from work

- recognise that the collection and use of information about an employee's health will have an adverse impact as it will represent an intrusion into that person's privacy

- ensure that policies, procedures and practices associated with the collection and use of health information about employees are no more intrusive than is necessary to meet the employer's stated business objectives

- restrict medical testing, for example by targeting certain forms of medical testing only at those who work in safety-critical jobs (rather than testing everyone), or designing medical testing to disclose only the minimum amount of health information that is required for the purpose for which the testing was undertaken

- keep sickness records separately from absence records (see below under 'Distinguishing between sickness and absence records').

Taking into account the second data protection principle (the duty to obtain personal data only for specified and lawful purposes) and the third principle (the duty to ensure that data is adequate, relevant and not excessive in relation to its purpose or purposes), it will be essential for the employer to ensure that all health information collected and retained on employees' files is held for a specific, legitimate business purpose, and that the type of information gathered is directly relevant to that purpose and not excessive when viewed against the purpose.

The sorts of purposes for which health information may legitimately be gathered and held would include measures to:

- ensure workplace safety

- determine whether employees meet eligibility requirements for certain employment benefits, for example a permanent health insurance scheme

- meet the employer's statutory duty to make reasonable adjustments for disabled employees

- process the payment of occupational and statutory sick pay

- manage attendance, thereby reducing the employer's sick pay costs.

Carrying out an impact assessment

The Employment Practices Data Protection Code on workers' health recommends that employers should conduct an impact assessment to ascertain whether there is justification for holding information about their employees' health. Through the impact assessment, the employer should aim to:

- ascertain the purpose(s) for which health information would be collected and the likely benefits of collecting it

- identify any likely adverse impact on employees of collecting and holding the information

- consider alternatives, that is whether there might be less intrusive ways of achieving these purposes

- decide objectively whether there is justification for collecting information about employees' health, and if so how much information needs to be collected (rather than just collecting information and assuming it is necessary).

The underlying principle is that employers should always consider carefully whether there is a real need to collect and hold health information about their employees, and if so, what level of detail is necessary to meet their business interests. Assuming there is justification for processing health data, the Code suggests, the employer should still seek to keep the collection and retention of such data to a minimum.

Distinguishing between sickness and absence records

Part 2 of the Employment Practices Data Protection Code, which deals with employment records, recommends that employers should keep sickness records separately from absence records.

- Sickness records will:
    - contain information about employees' physical or mental health
    - be highly personal and private to the individual
    - be classed as sensitive data under the Data Protection Act.

- Absence or attendance records will:
    - contain information about the dates of employees' absences from work and their frequency and duration
    - state only whether the absence was attributable to sickness or injury without providing any detail about employees' health or medical conditions
    - not be classed as sensitive data under the Data Protection Act.

In many cases, all that HR or line managers will need to fulfil their management responsibilities is data about absences, rather than information about an employee's health.

The Code of Practice suggests that employers should, wherever possible, use absence records rather than sickness records.

When health information constitutes sensitive data under the Data Protection Act

Data about employees' physical and mental health falls into the category of sensitive data under the Data Protection Act 1998. This means that employers must abide by certain fairly rigorous restrictions applicable to the processing of such data.

Conditions for the processing of health information

In order for it to be lawful for an employer to gather and retain information about an individual's health (which is classed as sensitive data under the Data Protection Act), the employer must ensure that at least one of a list of prescribed conditions is met. The conditions, which are set out on Schedule 3 to the Act allow employers to process sensitive data where:

- the individual about whom data is held has given explicit consent to the processing of the data (see below under 'Gaining employees' consent to the collection and use of health information')

- processing is necessary in order for the employer to exercise or perform a legal right or obligation in connection with employment, for example to comply with health and safety legislation or the duty under the Social Security Contributions and Benefits Act 1992 to process statutory sick pay for employees who are absent from work due to sickness

- processing is necessary to protect the vital interests of the employee or another person in circumstances where the employee cannot give consent or the employer cannot reasonably obtain consent, for example in the event of a serious medical emergency

- the information has been made public as a result of steps taken by the employee, for example where someone has been raising funds to support research into a particular medical condition and in so doing has made it public that he or she suffers from the condition in question

- processing is necessary in connection with any legal proceedings, for example in order to defend of a claim of disability discrimination brought against the employer at a tribunal, or is necessary for the purpose of obtaining legal advice

- processing is necessary for the exercise of any functions conferred under an enactment or of any functions of the Crown, a Minister of the Crown or a government department (likely to be relevant mainly to public sector employers)

- where processing is necessary for medical purposes and is undertaken by a health professional or someone with an equivalent duty of confidentiality.

This last condition would be applicable where health information about employees was held by an occupational doctor, nurse or similar health professional. It would not, however, apply to health data held by HR professionals or line managers. In respect of this condition, the Act further explains that 'medical purposes' include the purposes of preventative medicine, medical diagnosis, medical research, the provision of care and treatment, and the management of healthcare services.

It is important to note that, in order for data processing to be lawful, it must actually be necessary for the employer to hold the health data in question in order to fulfil the relevant condition. Holding health information about individuals as a matter of convenience or preference will not therefore satisfy the requirements of the Act.

Gaining employees' consent to the collection and use of health information

Unless one of the specific conditions listed above is met (see 'Conditions for the processing of health information' above), the employer will not be able lawfully to hold health data about an employee. The first of the conditions is that the individual has given consent to the processing of the data. In order for this condition to be satisfied, the consent must be explicit and freely given. 'Explicit' in this context means that the employee must have signed a document that clearly indicates that he or she has consented, while for that consent to be 'freely given', it must be clear that the employee genuinely had a choice as to whether or not to consent.

While it is therefore in the employer's interests to obtain each employee's signature on an appropriately worded document indicating clear consent to the collection and use of health data, it must be equally clear that the consent was given willingly, and not under pressure or under threat that some disadvantage might occur if the employee refused to consent.

Genetic testing

It is not recommended that employers should undertake compulsory genetic testing as a means of protecting their own or their employees' interests. Genetic testing is at a relatively early stage of development and is in most cases not a reliable means of predicting whether an individual will develop a particular condition during his or her working life. Furthermore, genetic testing will not be able to predict how severely a particular individual might be affected by the condition in question if it were to develop. For these reasons, and also for human rights reasons, it would be wholly inappropriate to base recruitment or employment decisions on genetic testing.

The only exception to this general principle could be where the employee is working in an environment where there are specific known risks, for example if the job involves contact with chemical substances. Even in these circumstances, genetic testing would only be potentially justifiable where:

- The particular factor in the workplace was known to pose a specific risk to people with a particular genetic variation.

- The reason for the test was to alert the employer and the employee that the employee might be placed at a higher than usual risk by working in a particular environment.

- The type of test used was known to be reliable in detecting the genetic condition in question.

Even if these three conditions could be met, it would be difficult to establish with any level of certainty that there was a tangible link between the particular workplace factor and the employee's susceptibility to it.

Conducting genetic testing would of course represent an extreme intrusion into the individual's private life and would therefore breach the individual's rights under Article 8 of the Human Rights Act 1998 (see above under 'Human rights and data protection implications'). Such an extreme level of intrusion would not normally be justifiable in the context of employment.

In addition to the relevant provisions of the Human Rights Act 1998, any records created or held as a result of testing would be classed as sensitive data under the Data Protection Act 1998 and be subject to the provisions of Part 4 of the Employment Practices Data Protection Code. The Code recommends that genetic testing should:

- never be used in an attempt to predict an employee's future general health

- not be used except as a last resort, that is, in circumstances where there is no other way for the employer to minimise a particular risk to health inherent in the workplace

- only be considered if there is reliable scientific evidence that the test to be deployed is valid in relation to the purpose for which the employer wishes to use it

- be done on a voluntary basis only, in circumstances where any potential risk is to the employee rather than to other staff.

The Code states further that employers who do conduct genetic testing should communicate the results of any test done directly to the employee who was tested and have arrangements in place to provide him or her with professional advice in the event that the test revealed a susceptibility to a particular condition.

POINTS TO NOTE

- There are many legitimate reasons why an employer may wish to obtain a medical report about an employee's health and fitness to work.

- Where an employer wishes to set up a meeting with someone who is absent from work due to sickness, it is advisable, if in doubt, to seek advice from an occupational doctor as to whether the employee is well enough to attend the particular meeting.

- The employer should exercise caution (but not necessarily back off altogether) if an employee alleges that the prospect of a meeting will cause stress or otherwise exacerbate the illness.

- It may be helpful for an employer to obtain medical advice in respect of an employee who has frequently been off work for short periods in order to ascertain or confirm whether there is any underlying medical condition causing the absences.

- The right of an individual under the Human Rights Act 1998 to respect for their privacy is not an absolute right, but stands to be balanced proportionally against the rights and freedoms of others.

- In order to be able to obtain a medical report from an employee's GP (but not normally one from an occupational doctor) the employer will need to abide by the provisions of the Access to Medical Reports Act 1988.

- Whenever an employer collects or holds any information about employees' health or sickness absence, the provisions of the Data Protection Act 1998 will apply.

- Data about employees' physical and mental health falls into the category of sensitive data under the Data Protection Act and is therefore subject to rigorous restrictions.

- Employees and other workers have a range of rights under the Data Protection Act, including the right be given a copy of any data held about them on request.

- Part 4 of the Employment Practices Data Protection Code (which covers data on workers' health) covers a range of issues, including occupational health data, medical testing, drug screening and genetic testing.

- The Code on workers' health recommends that employers should conduct an impact assessment to ascertain whether there is justification for holding information about their employees' health.

- In order for it to be lawful for an employer to gather and retain information about an employee's health, the employer must either obtain the individual's explicit consent or ensure that another condition from a prescribed list of conditions contained in the Data Protection Act is met.

- It is not recommended that employers should undertake compulsory genetic testing as a means of protecting their own or their employees' interests.

ACTION POINTS

- Adopt a flexible approach to the timing and location of any meeting with an employee who is off work sick.

- Refrain from jumping to negative conclusions about an employee who has frequent absences, as it may be that he or she is simply more prone than most people to common ailments such as colds and flu.

- View medical examinations as an opportunity to provide both the employer and the employee with a sound and fair basis for discussion if the employee's absences start to become excessive and/or cause operational problems for the employer.

- Ensure that any policy on requiring employees to submit to medical examinations has a specific, justifiable purpose, and that the type of medical examination required is proportionate (i.e. not excessive in relation to that purpose).

- Include a clause in every contract to the effect that the employee must consent to attend a medical examination with an occupational doctor nominated by the employer when asked to do so.

- Provide sufficient meaningful information to any doctor from whom a medical report about an employee is sought, and ask specific relevant questions of the doctor, so that he or she can make a reasoned judgment on the employee's fitness to work.

- Respect employees' rights under the Access to Medical Reports Act 1988, including their right to refuse to agree to allow the employer to apply to their GP for a medical report.

- If an employee refuses to agree to a medical examination or the provision of a medical report, explain clearly any possible consequences of that refusal to cooperate, particularly if dismissal on grounds of long-term ill-health absence has become a serious option.

- Adhere to the eight data protection principles contained in Schedule 1 of the Data Protection Act 1998.

- Review objectively whether the collection and use of health data about employees is necessary, and identify the specific purpose or purposes for which it is required.

- Comply with the recommendations contained in Part 4 of the Employment Practices Data Protection Code, as compliance with the Code should ensure compliance with the Data Protection Act.

- Ensure that all health information collected and retained on employees' files is held for a specific, legitimate business purpose, and that the type of information gathered is directly relevant to that purpose and not excessive when viewed against the purpose.

- Distinguish between sickness and absence records and keep the two separately.

INDEX